RULERS OF INDIA

RULERS OF INDIA

Madhava Rao Sindhia

AND THE HINDU RECONQUEST OF INDIA

H. G. KEENE, C.I.E., M. A.

GYAN

Published by

Gyan Publishing House
5, Ansari Road
Daryaganj, New Delhi-110002
Phone: 011-47034999, 9811692060
E-mail: books@gyanbooks.com

Distribution Network
gyanbooks.com
India, USA, Canada, UK, Australia, France

ISBN: 978-81-212-8466-0 (PB)
First Published, 1901

2nd Impression 2023

Printed at: Gyan Press, Delhi.

RULERS OF INDIA
Author: H. G. KEENE

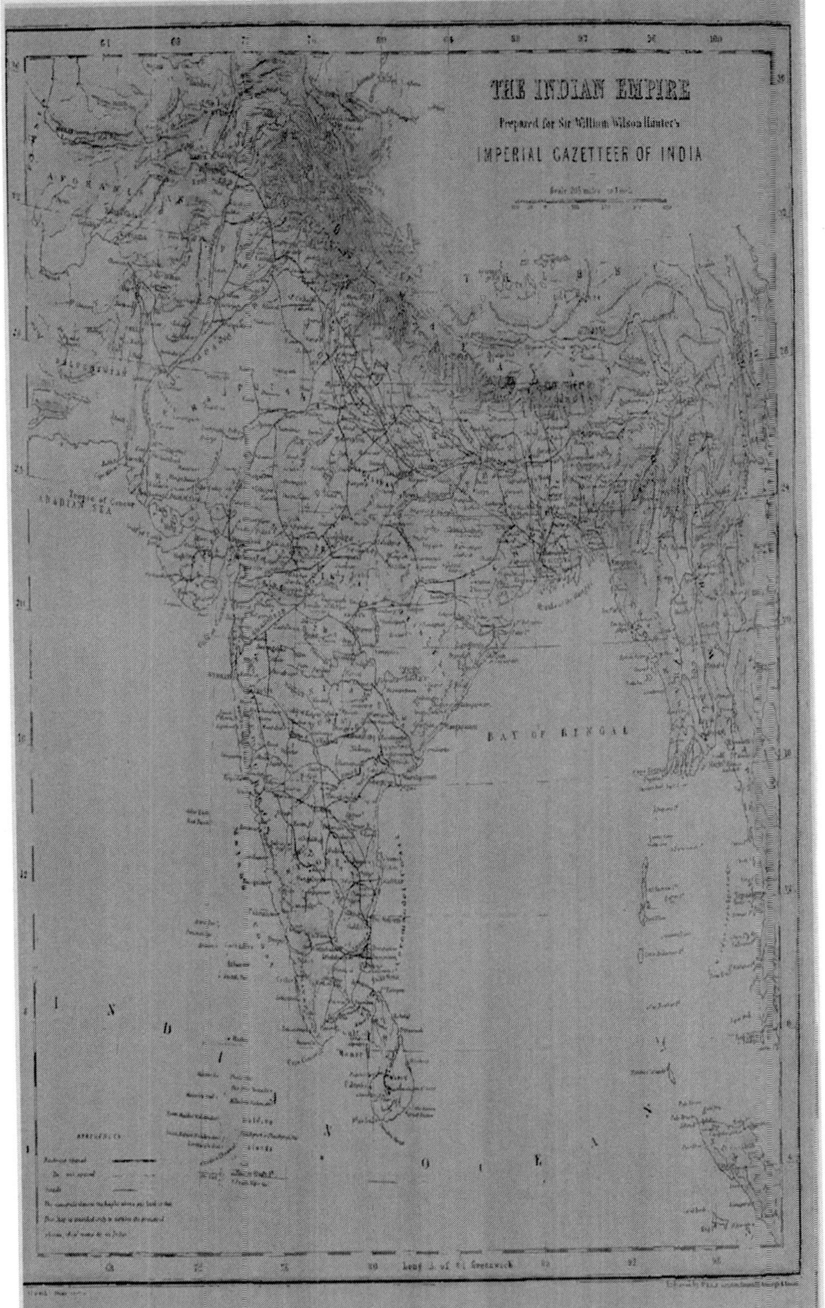
THE INDIAN EMPIRE
Prepared for Sir William Wilson Hunter's
IMPERIAL GAZETTEER OF INDIA
ARABIAN SEA
BAY OF BENGAL

RULERS OF INDIA

Mádhava Ráo Sindhia

AND THE HINDÚ RECONQUEST OF INDIA

By H. G. KEENE, C.I.E., M.A.

FOURTH THOUSAND

Oxford

AT THE CLARENDON PRESS; 1901

CONTENTS

NOTE

The orthography of proper names follows the system adopted by the Indian Government for the *Imperial Gazetteer of India*. That system, while adhering to the popular spelling of very well-known places, such as Punjab, Poona, Deccan, &c., employs in all other cases the vowels with the following uniform sounds :—

a, as in w*o*man : *á*, as in f*a*ther : *i*, as in k*i*n : *í*, as in intr*i*gue : *o*, as in c*o*ld : *u*, as in b*u*ll : *ú*, as in r*u*le.

PREFACE

In the following pages an attempt has been made to interest the reader in a remote and, at first sight, unattractive subject. The excuse is hinted on the title-page. The man of whom we treat was an Indian ruler of exceptional capacity in times of exceptional difficulty. Born before the sack of Delhi by Nádir Sháh he lived to within ten years of Lord Lake's occupation of the same imperial city. His life, therefore, exactly corresponds to the hour between the darkness of anarchy and the dawn of order, while his labours helped to make it pass. Himself a lover of order, he did what in him lay to clear away the worst havoc of war and rapine, and the consequent demoralisation: and to prepare the shattered fabric of society for restoration and reform. Hindustán, by which we are to understand the Northern Provinces of the Mughal Empire, had for a time been civilised and prosperous. Tavernier, writing about 1669, speaks of Sháh Jahán, then lately dead, as 'that great king during whose reign there was such a strictness in the civil government, and particularly for the security of the highways, that there was never any occasion to put any man to death for robbery.' A hundred years later it was observed that 'The country was torn to pieces by civil wars and groaned under every species of domestic confusion. Villainy was practised in every form; all law and religion were trodden under foot, the bonds of private friendship and connection, as well as of society and government, were broken; and every individual, as if in the midst of a forest of wild beasts, could rely upon nothing but the strength of his own arm.' (Dow; quoting native authority.) Such was the moral chaos that had followed the decline of the Empire; and, if the British rule has obliterated those marks of ruin and brought back civilisation, it is in some degree to Sindhia that the subjects of that rule are indebted for the first preparatory step.

Short as is the narrative, it has been found impossible to avoid the introduction of some extraneous matter. A mere biographical memoir, even if the materials of such were forthcoming, would not convey much instruction or pleasure to the reader. The French historical doctrine of the *milieu* may have been somewhat over-indulged of late years. In Mr. Russell Lowell's *Essay on Milton* we have an amusing account of a learned Professor's biography of that poet; in which historical pages are rarely diversified by occasional appearances of Milton: and the accomplished critic says that the reader is only reconciled when he calls to mind that this fair-haired stranger is, in fact, the protagonist. In the drama before us the protagonist is almost identified with the scenes in which he moved and the events in which he bore an influential part. He belongs at once to the faded Court of the Mughals and to the busy camp of the Maráthás: and the whole of his career is visible in the light of such relations. A man like Sindhia has no private life; and to understand what he was we must be shown what he did.

We must therefore endeavour to realise what was the Empire at whose agony our hero assisted and to whose estate he, for a time, administered; and we must seek some samples of the anarchy from which he delivered Hindustán. At the same time, we shall have to remember that Sindhia was not, originally, a native of Hindustán; and we must study, however briefly, the nature of that strange community in Southern India which, taking up the lapsed greatness of the old kingdom of Karnáta, almost succeeded in uniting the entire Indian peninsula in a universal Hindu Empire.

To do all this requires that we should be prepared to find copious and variegated materials digested into a result which may be found undesirably narrow. A small book may be found hard to read—as it, proverbially, is to write.

Our foundations have gone wide if not deep. Among the authorities to which those desirous of further information, or extended treatment, may profitably refer, may be named the undermentioned:—

(1) *History of the Mahrattas.* James Grant Duff. 3 vols. 1826.

(2) *Memoir of Central India.* Sir John Malcolm. 2 vols. 1820.

(3) *Memoirs of Col. Jas. Skinner, C.B.* Baillie Fraser. 2 vols. 1851.

(4) *Mémoire du Comte de Boigne* (by his son). Chambéri. 1829.

(5) *Síar-ul-mutákharín* (Ghulám Hosain Khán, translated by a French Creole employed in the office of Warren Hastings: his name was Raymond, and his notes are interesting). 3 vols.

(6) *Tárikh-i-Muzafari.* (Untranslated MS. by a Muhammadan gentleman in the service of the famous Muhammad Raza Khán, Naib Súba of Bihár, whose title, 'Muzafar Jang,' is preserved in the title.) Some account of these works will be found in Dowson's *Elliot*, viii.

(7) Col. Malleson's *Final French Struggles* (London, 1884) gives a good account of the doings of Gen. de Boigne and some of the minor European adventurers.

(8) Constant reference is made in the text to the *Imperial Gazetteer of India*; and the spelling of Oriental words is taken, generally, from the spelling adopted in the xivth vol., or Index, of that valuable work.

[The account of the campaign of 1760–1 is chiefly derived from the narrative of Pandit Kási Rái (iii, *Asiatic Researches*, 91 ff.). The writer was a

Secretary of the Oudh Nawáb, and present, both in the preliminary negotiations and on the field of battle: his description is remarkable as a unique narrative of military events by a Hindu civilian [1].

In Forrest's *Selections from the State-papers of the Government of India*, 3 vols., Calcutta, 1890, will be found a valuable series of minutes and despatches by Warren Hastings. See, also, Captain Trotter's monograph in this series.]

[1] A detailed account of the campaign, based on a collation of this and other contemporary narratives, will be found in my *Fall of the Moghul Empire* (3rd edition, 1887). Holkar's point of view will be seen to have been occasionally taken in Grant Duff (vol. ii, pp. 140–156).

The omission to cite Tod's *Rajasthan* may be thought to demand explanation. It is a noble book, full of priceless information and inspired by a fine enthusiasm. But this very inspiration renders the author an unsafe guide in regard to the relations and dealings of the Rájputs with other tribes.

PEDIGREE OF THE SINDHIA FAMILY.

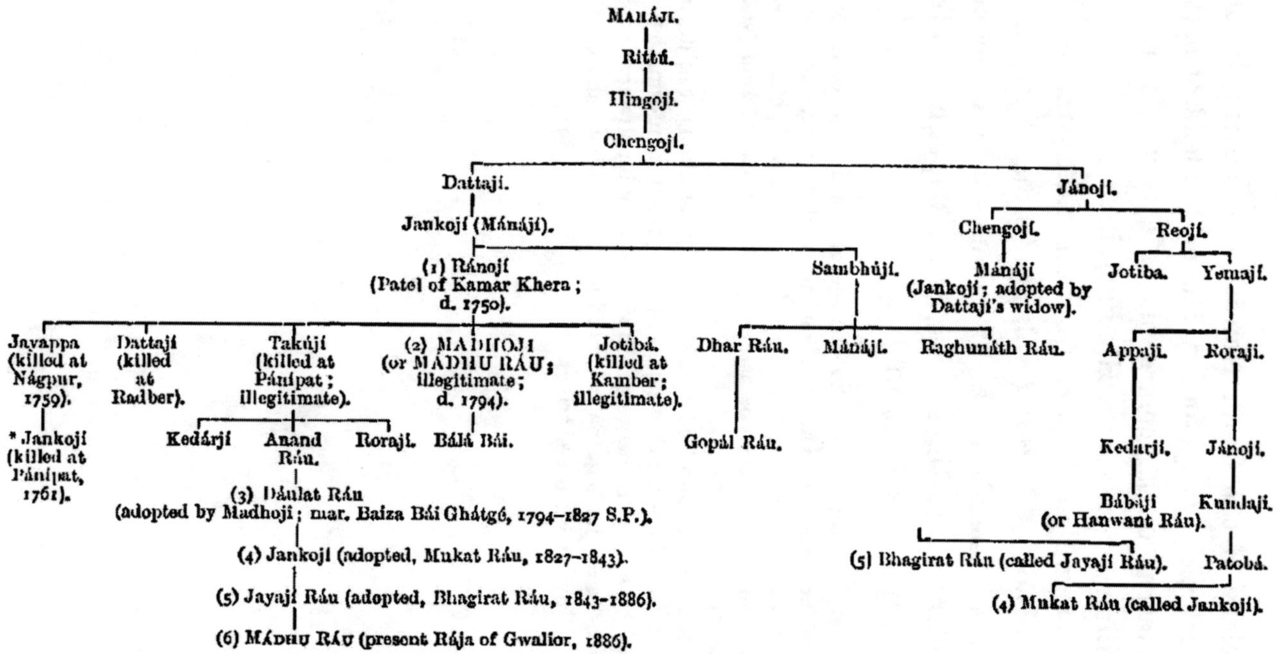

* Jankojí appears to have led the Sindhia clan in the disastrous campaign of 1760–1 in virtue of primogeniture. After his death Madhoji was the only adult representative of Ránojí Patel who was left. (Malcolm, *Central India*, 2nd Ed. I. 118.)

CHAPTER I

INTRODUCTORY

THE Hindu confederacy of which the subject of this book was, in his time, a prominent member, indicates an episode in that perennial struggle which has been going on for eight centuries in India between the social and religious system of the Hindus and that of their Musalmán compatriots. Neither Musalmán nor Hindu society can be considered 'national,' though, as earlier conquerors who have associated and assimilated with the original inhabitants, the Hindus naturally appear now to represent whatever may be found at all deserving the name of an Indian nationality.

Maháráshtra, meaning the tract bounded on the west by the ocean, on the north by the Narbadá, on the east by the Waingangá, and on the south by the Krishna rivers, was a Hindu kingdom in the time of Hiuen Tsiang, the Chinese pilgrim (640 A.D.), of which the capital was at Kalyáni, or Kalyán, near the modern city of Bombay. In the sixteenth century the Portuguese obtained a considerable footing in Maháráshtra, of which fragments are still in existence, notably the town and territory of Goa. The people, however, had been known for some time from the name of their country: for the name *Marhat* occurs in the history of Sultán Juna (or Muhammad Tughlak) who invaded Southern India in the middle of the fourteenth century; and before long we find mention of them in connection with the Musalmán kingdom of Bijapur. Yusaf 'Adil Sháh, the first of the 'Adil Sháhi dynasty, is said to have given command of 12,000 infantry to a Hindu Chief from that country; and in the reigns of his successors they freely shared in public employment. They were known as light cavalry, and they seem to have taught the Bijapur Musalmáns that system of guerilla warfare to which the kingdom owed its ability to resist its enemies for nearly two hundred years.

So much has this system of war been celebrated that we have fallen into a way of thinking of the people of Maháráshtra as all homogeneous and a mere tribe of predatory riders. The facts, however, do not altogether affirm this view. On the contrary we find them divided, like Hindu societies elsewhere, into distinct classes: the Bráhmans, who have been the most distinguished in public affairs; an ordinary class of fighting men claiming to be descended from Rájput immigrants; the *Kunbis*, or agriculturists; and a mixed multitude of townsmen and artisans, often called, locally, *Shankarjáti*, probably sprung from marriages between the pure Hindu immigrants and the aboriginal women. Their state appears to have at once adopted the character of a federal commonwealth and a military monarchy; where the king was assisted by Bráhman counsellors, and the rural *Communes* sent the flower of their young men to serve in a more or less embodied militia. These peasant warriors were despised by the arrogant and luxurious Muhammadans, both for their lack of pomp and splendour, and for something business-like and unchivalrous in their manner of fighting. But those were the very qualities which led to the first successes of the people of Maháráshtra when the Musalmán power ran to seed. Could the Mughals have stayed their own degeneracy, and at the same time could they have employed the Maráthás as the Cossacks and Uhlans of their unwieldy armies, they might have used them with irresistible effect in the conquest of the Deccan; and might, possibly, have succeeded in the scheme, in itself not unreasonable, of consolidating the whole peninsula of India into one Empire.

But *Dîs aliter visum*; and when the great but mistaken attempt of the Emperor 'Alamgír, commonly known as Aurangzeb, had ended in disaster, the destruction of the southern Musalmán kingdoms only swept a clear field for the Maráthá enterprise. Then they found the opportunity for which they had been so long waiting: they adopted wider aims, and a more imposing style; adding to their direct possessions while they extended their indirect sway and influence in every direction. As this extension proceeded they organised their habits of levying contribution on the subjects of other States. At last their system of tribute came to spread over almost the whole of the peninsula. It was not so much an Empire as an Anti-empire. Let others, they seemed to say, undertake the task of administration and of watching for the welfare of the multitude. They will be making honey not for themselves; on their most prosperous towns and parishes, we will, without unnecessary violence or mischief, make our regular and understood claim of twenty-five per cent. of the revenues, surely not an exorbitant commission for abstaining from disturbing their enjoyment of life and property. 'Do thou,' said Virgil, 'remember, O Roman, to rule the peoples.' The *Pax Maratica* was founded on the opposite principle:—'Take pay for not ruling.'

The modern power of this extraordinary race arose in the reign of the Emperor Sháh Jahán, and owed its origin to the strenuous efforts of that Mughal monarch to annex the territory of Bijápur and abolish its sovereignty. We need not here go into the detailed history of the Bijápur State; it will be enough to say that it grew out of a satrapy of the old Southern Musalmán Empire of the so-called 'Bahmani' dynasty, which became independent under a Turkmán governor named Yusaf 'Adil about the end of the fifteenth century A.D. In the time of Sháh Jahán the nominal ruler was a minor, and the Regency was for some time held by a Maráthá captain, named Sháhjí Bhonslá, who aided the Emperor to overthrow the neighbouring power of the Nizám Sháh, at Ahmadnagar, and is famous as the founder of the family afterwards elevated to a brief but bright eminence by his son. Sháhjí's great title to distinction is that he was the father of the still more distinguished Sivají.

That remarkable man went early to a far greater length than his father; possessed himself of forts, organised a regularly-paid army, both horse and foot, and finally assumed the functions and insignia of a king. He shook off his connection with Bijápur and with the Mughals; and laid the foundation of that inveterate system of depredation and hostility which, under his successor, finally wore out the courage of Aurangzeb and introduced the germ of decay into his empire. His grandson, having been in his youth a captive at court, adopted Mughal manners: and the power of the State fell into the hands of a dynasty of Bráhman ministers under whom the civil administration became organised, and the military system was raised to much pomp and splendour. The robes of empire now hung not ungracefully on the limbs of a Hindu, and one of two things was bound to happen; either there would be a new empire, doomed to rise and fall after the usual manner, or a federal India must be born, under the protection of a new and foreign power. The subject of the present narrative becomes the necessary man of an epoch of transition when this point was still undetermined; a transition between guerilla foraging and scientific war.

Mádhava Ráo, or 'Madhoji,' Sindhia has been

described, on good authority, as 'a statesman and soldier of almost unsurpassed ability' (*Imp. Gazetteer of India*, v. 230). He rose to rule in Hindustán without altogether losing touch with the distant and difficult politics of the Maráthá State. Like other unusually successful men, he was partly the child of his time and partly its creator. Ordinary average success is often produced by the qualities of the commoner class, such as docility and power of adaptation; but this man's was another, and a fairer kind of success. He changed the habits of men, gave a new direction to their thoughts, and prepared a social revolution. He did so because his aims were clear and reasonable, definitely conceived and resolutely pursued, without ignoring the continuity of human interests.

But, before proceeding to support these claims by an examination of Mádhava's record, it will be desirable to say a few words concerning the scene on which he played his part, and the events which preceded his appearance. India, in his time, was 'a geographic expression,' just as, then and long after, was the case with Italy. The Alpine and Subalpine region of the peninsula was peopled by hardy races with whom he, as much as possible, avoided contact. From the Sutlej river to the Narbadá is a bilateral region sending mighty streams to the Arabian sea and the bay of Bengal. Within its points are old nations, with their forts, and cities, and fields, where the shepherd and the husbandman contend as in the days of Cain and Abel. Beyond the Narbadá is a further region of hill and plain and river, inhabited by races of less contentious habits and a more recent civilisation. In both of these last-named regions our hero played a conspicuous part for more than a generation.

India's three great natural divisions, thus hastily delineated, are described by modern European geographers as cardinal sections; and they are, moreover, known to Orientals; by whom, however, they are more usually subdivided, the subdivisions being called by many names. The first contains several regions; omitting Afghánistán, Kashmír, and the Punjab, which will not enter into our narrative, there remain two to be specified in the lower, or alluvial, portion. The northernmost is known as Hindustán, a name often given by Europeans to the whole peninsula, but reserved by the natives to the tract bordered on the north by the Sutlej river, and on the south by the Chambal. Its eastern slope, between the Ganges and the Jumna, is known as the Doáb, or, as might be said in Latin, 'Mesopotamia,' but it also includes the Trans-Gangetic Provinces of Katahr (or Rohilkhand) and Oudh. South of the Chambal, and partially draining to the west, is the hill-country of the Arávalli and Vindhya ranges, in whose embraces lie the states of the Rájputs, old tribes of the Hindus driven thither before the early Musalmán invaders. To the east of these, and southward to the Narbadá, the country is called Central

India; and here lie the original fiefs of Málwá and Gwalior, acquired in the eighteenth century by the clans of Sindhia and Holkar and still held by the respective chiefs of those Houses. Still further to the eastward lie the minor provinces of Bhopál and Bundelkhand. The last region is south of the Narbadá, called in history 'The Deccan'; containing likewise many provinces, divided by limits which have fluctuated as one dynasty or tribe has advanced or receded[1].

Nevertheless, throughout this vast and varied peninsula, a tendency towards union has been observed in many stages of its history. Mythical monarchies of all India had floated vaguely in popular tradition when, in the sixteenth century, one of those movements so frequent in cold countries drew the 'Mughals' from Kábul down upon the sunny south[2]. It cost them two hard struggles; but scarcely was their empire consolidated under the great Akbar when the idea was revived of 'bringing all India under one *chhatri*' (umbrella, the symbol of Empire).

The reduction of ambitious feudatories and rebellious officials once accomplished, the process began. Radiating from Agra and Delhi the emperors slowly extended their power: building their palaces at

[1] The name of 'Deccan' is as old as the Greek geographer Ptolemy. Etymologically, the word is *Dakhin* = 'South' ('right-hand' is the same in Sanskrit, and supposing the face to the East).

[2] For some account of this race and its conquests see the author's *Sketch of the History of Hindostan*.

Allahábád, Ajmere, Lahore, and Kashmír. Nevertheless, the Rájput Chiefs remained, as they remain to this day, virtually autonomous in their remote fastnesses; though two of their States became completely friendly and even feudatory to the Empire, showing the sincerity of their submission by giving their noblest sons to command in the Imperial armies and their fairest daughters to furnish brides for the Imperial households. In the Deccan, likewise, the Imperial arms made some genuine progress. The old Hindu kingdoms of that region had broken up, between the fourteenth and the sixteenth centuries, to be succeeded by a number of Musalmán States which the Mughals, from Akbar onwards, were constantly battering and shattering, first reducing them to the tributary condition, and then rendering them mere dependencies.

In 1637 a further step was taken: Sháh Jahán, the grandson of Akbar, destroying the Nizám Sháhi dynasty of Ahmadnagar by complete annexation of the state over which that dynasty had ruled for nearly two centuries. In 1686 his son, 'Alamgír, commonly known to Europeans as 'Aurangzeb,' carried on the same process against the 'Adil Sháhi dynasty of Bijapur. In the following year the last of the great Musalmán States was overthrown, that of the Kutab-Sháhi line in Golconda. The area of these conquered kingdoms went to form the new province, or *Súbah*, of the Deccan, great part of which is still held, under the Sovereignty of the Queen Empress, by the powerful vassal of the Crown who is popularly known as 'the Nizám,' and who is descended from the first Viceroy who shook off his dependence on the Empire. For it should be observed that, as the extension of the Mughal Empire was made without adequate means, so the process of integration was interrupted as soon as the central power began to relax; and the contrary process of disintegration almost instantaneously set in, and acted with extreme rapidity. As happened a thousand years ago in the somewhat analogous case of the Karling Empire of Europe, each great satrapy became a separate nation in less than two generations after the Empire attained its full extent.

The mention of these satrapies suggests another comparison. The Mughal Empire of India is, chronologically, not very far remote from modern times. It was seen in its glory by a school-fellow of Molière; the description of its glories fired the imagination of Milton; its palace-halls, but a few years ago, made ball-rooms for the present Heir-apparent to the British Empire; its last representative has not been long dead. Yet that Empire was, in all essential characteristics, a fragment of the ancient world; a counterpart, in all but its religious system, of the mighty monarchies of Babylon and Persia. There was the same awe-breathing distance between the grovelling subject and the exalted despot; the same sinister contrast between the squalor of the cottage and the splendour of the throne; the might of the monarch was haunted by the menace of the remote rebel and the shadow of the domestic traitor. In such an Empire there could be no 'Act of Settlement' or 'Responsibility of Cabinets'; but the sovereign, after a longer or shorter period of uncontrolled despotism, falls into the insanity of power or drivels into the dotage of decay. Provinces fall off from their allegiance, the despot crushes, or is crushed; at last he disappears, perhaps killed in battle, perhaps poisoned in a palace-intrigue. He is succeeded by a courtier, a slave, or one of his own fratricidal sons; and the hideous business begins anew. In such revolutions the Empire is often weakened, sometimes quite dissolved. In its incoherent way, however, it comes together again, some old parts lost, some new members gained; and once more the booty of conquered neighbours and the wealth wrung from helpless subjects are concentrated on the person and palace of the ruler. It is still a shifting scene of contrast, the monarch of one moment becomes the victim of another, or the puppet of an able minister. But always there remains the sinister glare of unbridled luxury and unprofitable decoration. The autocrat —no better, saner, or happier than the meanest of his peasants—swathes his perishable frame in brocade and jewelry, and takes his daily seat upon a couch of gold[1]; surrounded by obsequious kinsmen and tributary princes. In ordered ranks beneath the

[1] The throne of an oriental monarch takes the form of a square bedstead, on which he sits with crossed legs.

elevated platform are marshalled the courtiers, ministers, generals, the chiefs of peace and war, and the messengers and representatives of those who are absent in the distant regions, ruling the provinces of the Empire or commanding its military forces. The same eternal picture was presented to Daniel the Hebrew, to Ctesias the Greek, to Tavernier the French jewel-merchant, and Bernier the correspondent of Colbert. The last-named traveller visited almost all the great Musalmán courts. He had seen the court of the 'Roi-Soleil,' the sumptuous Louis XIV, and those of the Sultáns of Syria and Egypt; and this is his account of the display that he found at that of the 'Great Mogul.'

'The king appeared, sitting upon his throne, in the bottom of the great hall of the *Am-kas*, splendidly apparelled. His vest was of white flowered satin and raised with a fine embroidery of gold and silk. His turban was of cloth of gold, having a bird worked upon it, like a heron, whose foot was covered with diamonds of an extraordinary bigness and value, with a great oriental topaz, which may be said to be matchless, shining like a miniature sun. A collar of great pearls hung about his neck and down to his breast, after the manner in which some of the heathen [Musalmáns] wear here their rosaries for prayer. His throne was supported on six high pillars, or feet, said to be of massive gold, and set with rubies, and emeralds, and diamonds. I am not able to tell you aright, either the number or the price of this mass of precious stones, because it is not possible to come near enough to count them or to judge of their purity and value. Only this I can say, that the big diamonds are there in profusion and that the throne is estimated to be worth four *krors* of rupis, each worth a *demi-ecu*[1].' [This was the 'Peacock Throne' of Sháh Jahán, the value of which, by Bernier's estimate, was £2,400,000; though Tavernier, an expert, afterwards doubled the sum.] 'So that the throne is valued at forty millions of rupis . . . about sixty millions of francs. . . Beneath there appeared all the *Omras* in splendid apparel upon a raised ground shaded by a great canopy of purfled gold-cloth with golden fringes, enclosed by a silver balister. The pillars of the hall were hung with tapestries, having a gold ground-work; and the ceiling was covered with canopies of flowered satin fastened with cords of red silk ornamented with tassels of silk, mixed with gold, that hung down from them.'

Such is Bernier's account of the throne and its surroundings. In another place he adds: 'Thence he sees beneath him the Lords, Rajas, and representative envoys, who are all standing upon a raised space enclosed with silver rails, with down-cast eyes and arms folded upon their breasts; somewhat further off he sees the lesser lords, or *Mansabdárs*, also standing in the like posture of reverence; and, somewhat

[1] The rupee of those days was therefore worth no more than fifteen pence.

further off still in the remaining part of the hall, and in the open court-yard, he can see a great crowd of the commonalty. For there it is that the king, every day about noon, gives universal audience.' This was a general levée, where the Bádsháh not only received his chiefs, but acted the old oriental part of the father of his people, sitting at his tent-door to administer justice. It need hardly be added that much of the pageant was symbolical; the sovereign's court was not a real court of law, and he had not much more personal connection with the administration than Her Majesty, with us, exercises in the 'Queen's Bench.' Nevertheless the peerage of the Amara and *Mansabdárs* mentioned by Bernier was a very real institution, and one whose reality contained an undoubted germ of development.

By 'omras' Bernier meant the courtiers, in especial favour and constant attendance, perhaps most conceivable to us as 'Ministers,' or 'Lords-in-waiting.' Their chief went by the title of *Amir-ul-amara*= premier noble, and was next to the Wazír in dignity; sometimes also in power, or even actually, in practice, superior. The *Mansabdárs* were nobles too, but of a more military character; whose rank was expressed by the number of men-at-arms that they were supposed to lead. In strict nomenclature these also were *amírs* if their patents were for more than 500 horsemen; above 5000 was the highest grade of all, reserved originally for princes of the blood. Of the ranks between these two limits there were, in Bernier's time, 580 nobles of which number about one-fifth consisted of Hindus, the remainder being either native Musalmáns or immigrants of distinction from Persia and Central Asia, known in India, though not very accurately, as 'Mughals.'

Ranking immediately after the princes of the blood and the great officials these mansabdárs formed a military peerage like the paladins of Charlemagne or Cromwell's Major-Generals. But their titles were not meant to be hereditary, such transmission of grandeur being quite opposed to oriental notions. A blacksmith or a water-carrier, there, has sometimes risen to the command of armies; a successful slave has often ascended the throne at whose foot he once ministered. The sons of deceased *amírs* might have an indefinite right to employment, but it would never be in the command of their father's *mansabs*: the best that they could expect would be to begin life as *ahdis*, or unattached cavaliers, perhaps with a slender following, perhaps, if they were very poor, alone: these gentlemen-cadets would at first rank as private troopers, but would be excused from sentry and fatigue-duties, until they were deemed worthy of promotion. A choice body of *ahdis* formed the mounted body-guard of the monarch [1].

The last class of attendants at the levee described by Bernier, was that whose French designation has been translated above as 'Envoys'; the *Vakils*, or

[1] Corresponding to the 'Exempts' of the old French monarchy, a name preserved in the 'Exons' of the Queen's body-guard.

Agents, of those Amírs who were absent on distant service. The Empire was divided, in those days, into fifteen provinces, each being administered by a lord-deputy, like Ireland under Elizabeth, and still more like Satrapies of the old Empires. Each of these viceroys had his own smaller court, a mimic reproduction of the sovereign's; but each was liable to transfer or removal from office during his lifetime. The first Nizám was at one time appointed to Rohilkhand, at another translated to Málwá; it was not till the second quarter of the eighteenth century that he was able to construct a hereditary principality out of his last viceroyship in the Deccan. In all this constitution we are reminded of nothing so much as of 'King Ahasuerus on the throne in Shushan the palace, with his princes and servants; the power of Persia and Media, and the nobles of the provinces being before him; when he showed the riches of his kingdom; and there were hangings of white cloth, of green and of blue fastened with cords of purple to silver rings and pillars of marble, and the thrones were of gold and silver upon a pavement of porphyry and white marble and alabaster' [*Rev. Vers. of Bible*, Esther, i. 3, 6]. Here the provincial satraps would seem to have been in attendance: usually they would be represented by agents.

Such was the Mughal Empire in its palmy state. When Bernier left the country there appeared no symptom of decadence, unless a peculiarly shrewd observer might have noted the change in the personal character of the sovereign. Inferior to none of the great Sultáns, from whom he was descended, in courage or application, 'Alamgír, known to us by his private name 'Aurangzeb,' was, in some vital respects, unfit to carry on their system. With Hindu wives and mothers they had been tolerant, almost Catholic, in their ideas, and of jovial manners. The Emperor 'Alamgír was the son of a Persian mother, known in her lifetime for a fanatical and persecuting temper. The youngest of a large family, he had carved out his own fortunes by audacity, suspicion, and intrigue; of austere and frugal habits, he had greatly curtailed the expenses of the Court, had put down much of its traditional display, and even discontinued the biweekly appearance at the palace window where his predecessors had been accustomed to receive the respectful greetings of the common people. Finally, he pursued the dream of universal empire without the necessary accompaniments of conciliation, and revived the hated poll-tax upon his Hindu subjects which had been suspended ever since the days of Akbar; reminding us of his contemporary in France and the revocation of the Edict of Nantes.

Thus his conquests in the Deccan only encouraged Maráthá presumption and bred perpetual trouble; so that, when he was entombed at Aurangábád, in 1707, he had been to the last breath haunted by remorse and anxiety, by the disputes of his sons, and by the cares arising out of his annexations. At last, in 1713, the government of the new *Súbah* fell into the hands of

Hosain Alí, one of the king-making Saiads[1]. This man left the province in charge of his kinsmen while he directed the affairs at Delhi; the conception of forming a remote viceroyship into a dynastic principality, however unconstitutional, was obvious, as matters then went; and it was soon adopted by an abler aspirant. This was an official more resembling what in Europe is considered a man of high birth than is usual in Musalmán countries, being the son of Firoz Khán, a Turkmán of distinguished rank, who had held high commands in the Deccan for half a century. The son, originally known as Kamr-ud-din Khán, had assumed the title of 'Ásaf Jáh,' and the office of Prime Minister to the Emperor Muhammad Sháh, in January 1721. In a little more than three years he had thrown up in disgust an office which the levity of the young monarch hindered him from discharging to his satisfaction; and had repaired to the Deccan, where he founded the State which still subsists under the name of 'The Nizám's Dominions.' Nominally, it was the Súbah erected on the ruins of the old Musalmán kingdoms; but in the decline of the Empire it became a hereditary and quasi-independent province, though the ruler never took the royal title, but continued to retain the style of an Imperial Viceroy, as 'Nizám-ul-múlk,' which his descendant still bears.

[1] The 'Seiads' of Elphinstone, properly *Sayid* = 'a prince,' or 'descendant of the Prophet.' It is in this secondary sense alone that the word is used in India. The title of the famous 'Cid' of Spain is an instance of the primary meaning.

Ásaf Jáh was a valiant and prudent ruler. The Maráthás had been granted a tribute from the province, and this he was unable to withhold. But he succeeded in effecting an arrangement by virtue of which this tribnte was to be collected by his own officers and paid to the Maráthás out of his treasury, so that he saved the commission hitherto charged by the Maráthá collectors while his people were spared the visitations of a double collecting agency.

This, however, may be regarded as the culminating period of the Hindu ascendency in Maháráshtra. The civil administration was under a complete political hierarchy. The nominal head, under the Rájá, was a sort of chancellor, entitled *Pratinidhi*; but there was a council of state called the *Asht pardhán*, or 'Council of Eight,' of which the President, or *Mukh-pardhán*, bore the title of *Peshwá*; and, shortly before the foundation of the Nizám's power at Haidarábád the then Peshwá, Bálají Viswanáth, had, by conspicuous business abilities, become in effect the first person in the government. He died in 1720, and was succeeded by his eldest son, Bájí Ráo, who carried on his complicated system. The Pratinidhi, Sripat Ráo, maintained for some time his constitutional position as chief administrator; but being opposed to the extension of the Maráthá empire he lost influence; while the Peshwá, by giving his attention to military reform, fascinated both Rájá and people, and became by rapid degrees the leader of the confederacy. He was the first to show the path by which Mádhava

Sindhia afterwards rose to supremacy; the Mughal Empire, he said, was a withered trunk: let them strike at this and the boughs would fall of themselves. Accordingly, while retaining the twofold organisation of the cavalry[1], he reduced that force to a governable condition; while he established a body of infantry which, with a due proportion of guns, should give consolidation and steadiness to the army.

The first step in the ambitious projects to which Bájí Ráo committed his willing sovereign was the conquest of the rich province of Málwá. This, which had formed part of a former viceroyship of the Nizám, had been transferred by the Emperor to a Hindu Súbadár, Rájá Girdhar Rai, when the Nizám went to Haidarábád; and the enterprising Maráthá leader now proceeded to invade it with the connivance of the dispossessed Nizám. In the campaign which ensued, two of his principal officers were the *Silládárs*, or leaders of partisan horse, named, respectively, Malhárji Holkar and Ránojí Sindhia: and to them the Peshwá issued patents authorising them to levy the usual Maráthá tribute, and to retain a moiety for the payment of their troops. The war began in 1727; but was interrupted by a quarrel with the Nizám, of which the ultimate result was that the Peshwá got the better of his rivals; and, although the Nizám himself escaped ruin, the power of Bájí Ráo was

[1] *Bárgirs*, or paid horsemen, and *Silládárs*, or leaders of militia cavalry.

established as supreme in the Maráthá Government. The conquest of Málwá soon followed, as will be related presently.

The Peshwás henceforth became a dynasty of hereditary Presidents of the Confederacy, or United States, of Southern India. In 1751 the Maráthás had become masters of Málwá and Orissa, and drew their 25 per cent. from the revenues of Bengal. Calcutta, the British Factory, was threatened; and the 'Maráthá Ditch' was dug as a part of the works for its protection. It was the strengthening of these fortifications, indeed, which provoked the Mughal Nawáb five years later and led to the Black-Hole and all its momentous consequences.

Meanwhile the invasions of the Persians and Afgháns had brought the Court of Delhi to complete prostration. Then followed a chronic feud between the two great parties of immigrant nobles who contended for the wreck of the Empire. The Persian party, or 'Lords of Irán,' were headed by Safdar Jang, of Oudh, while the Turkmáns, or 'Lords of Túrán,' were led by a nephew of the Nizám, called Ghází-ud-dín. The Maráthás under Holkar joined with the Játs, on the side of the former party, but they were worsted. Ghází-ud-dín then deposed the Emperor, and proceeded to set up another Emperor, by the title of 'Alamgír II (1754).

The convulsions of the Muhammadan power in Hindustán were witnessed with sorrow by a great warrior of that faith, the famous Ahmad Sháh Abdáli, who had founded the Duráni Empire west of the Indus after the death of Nadír Sháh. At the head of a body of Afghán horsemen Ahmad, advancing from Kandahár, swept through the Punjab, and arrived at Delhi about the beginning of the year 1757. Accompanied by Najíb Khán—a Pathán Chief who was in secret correspondence with the invader—Ghází-ud-dín the Turkmán minister marched out to encounter the invader; and so complete was the isolation into which his character had brought him, that he only learned his true position when he beheld the greater part of his army follow Najíb into the enemy's lines, where they were received as expected guests. He then hastened to make his peace with the Abdáli; and gave him the aid of his officers and men in collecting from the Játs and other inhabitants of the surrounding country a tribute which could hardly be distinguished from plunder. Having, then, drained the citizens of Delhi of whatever had been left by Nadír Sháh the Afgháns departed in the beginning of winter. Before his departure their leader appointed Najíb to the post of *Amir-ul-Amara*, and enjoined upon him the duty of protecting the feeble old Emperor. But Ghází-ud-dín was too strong for the new minister, whom he expelled by force when Ahmad was well gone; and, incited by Ghází, a Maráthá force of cavalry under two of the sons of Ránojí Sindhia proceeded to attack Najíb in his own fief and hem him into Rokilkhand. Master of Delhi Ghází-ud-dín proceeded to oppress the Emperor and his family.

The Crown Prince, Alí Gauhar, saved himself by flight, but the infamous young Turkmán murdered the inoffensive Emperor (30 Nov. 1759). The fugitive Prince assumed the title of Bádsháh (Emperor) under the protection of Shujá-ud-daulá, the Nawáb of Oudh and hereditary Wazír of the Empire; and the Afghán leader returned to his cantonment of Anúpshahr, on the Upper Ganges. The Nawáb Wazír coalesced with Najíb to oppose the Maráthás; and Ghází-ud-dín, finding his position no longer tenable, took refuge with the Játs of Bhartpur [1].

[1] He died a fugitive and an outcast, about the year 1800.

CHAPTER II

Sindhia at Pánípat

It was mentioned above that in 1759 the Maráthás in Hindustán were under the command of two sons of Ránojí Sindhia. These were Dattáji and 'Madhoji,' or Mádhava Ráo, two young men who had already distinguished themselves against the French and their 'Nizám' in the war of 1751. Of the former of these we shall have nothing further to record: he endeavoured to secure the friendship of Najíb and the Rohillás in the event of any conflict with Ahmad Sháh that might be approaching; and he then went off to the Punjab accompanied by Malhár Ráo Holkar, to meet the Afgháns by whom they were defeated and forced to fly, though not till Dattáji had fallen.

The heart of the exhausted Empire had now almost ceased to beat. Never in modern times has a civilised country fallen into such a condition. The state of France during the Hundred Years War was bad enough, but there was still a centre of royalty and a spark of patriotic spirit left, among the governing classes, if the people at large had lost hope. Here, the ruin of the government had been gradual and soon became final. There was not only no class of society left to make head against foreign invasion, but there was none left to heal the wounds of the body politic when foreign invaders should depart. It may seem that we are witnessing a combat of kites and crows; but at least there is something tragic in the aspect of so vast and famous a land extended as a helpless prize for their contentions.

In the meantime the Deccan, though less inactive, was not much more prosperous. If Hindustán lay like a moribund carcase, the south of India flamed like a volcano. To compensate for the failure of his forces in the north, the new Peshwá, Bálají, had sent his cousin, Sheodásheo Ráo, commonly called 'the Bháo,' to attack the dominions of the Nizám. The Bháo soon obtained possession of the city of Ahmadnagar, and the surrounding country; and negotiations began by means of which the Nizám ultimately saved the remnant of his power though by painful sacrifices. Flushed with this success, the Bháo next proposed to carry out the design of the deceased Bájí Ráo, to drive the Musalmáns out of Hindustán and acquire the universal rule of India for the Maráthás. The scheme looked feasible. The Maráthá army no longer consisted merely of foraying spearmen and light guerilla riders; it included a large force of well-mounted cavalry drawing regular pay from the State, and a considerable body of infantry imbued with French discipline. Bájí Ráo's design seemed about to be realised

Among the foremost leaders of his army had been Ránojí Sindhia, who had risen from a humble position; who had been succeeded on his death by his grandson Jankojí; and whose illegitimate son, Mádhava, has been mentioned as operating in Hindustán when his brother Dattáji was killed by the Afgháns. Mádhava, born about 1730, now accompanied his nephew at the head of the contingent of cavalry furnished by the clan from their hereditary fief in Northern Málwá.

Flushed with the pride of youth and conquest the Bháo, accompanied by Viswás Ráo, son of the Peshwá, moved out of Poona in September, 1759, in all the pomp of a Mughal General: his camp, enriched with the plunder of the Deccan Musalmáns, was on a scale of splendour hitherto unknown to the Maráthás. 'The lofty and spacious tents,' says Grant Duff, 'lined with silks and broadcloths, were surmounted by great gilded ornaments, conspicuous at a distance ... Vast numbers of elephants, flags of all descriptions, the finest horses, magnificently caparisoned ... seemed to be collected from every quarter ... it was an imitation of the more becoming and tasteful array of the Mughals in the zenith of their glory.' Nor was this pomp the only innovation. Originally irregular horsemen, armed with long bamboo lances; carrying food, forage, bedding, and stable-gear; making sudden dashes on baggage-guards; galloping fifty miles after a repulse, and ready to form and fight again next day; the Maráthá horse now formed a compact body of 20,000 chosen cavaliers; with a train of artillery, and a division of

10,000 musketeers and gunners, disposed in battalions and field-batteries. This latter division was under a Musalmán soldier of fortune, named Ibráhím Gárdi: he had learned French discipline under Bussy, and took his second name from having commanded that officer's body-guard at Haidarábád, whence he had been discharged, and immediately engaged by the Bháo. Many Hindu Chiefs brought their irregular contingents to swell the progress of the advancing army. Holkar joined in Málwá, the Gáekwár led his men from Gujarát. From Bundelkhand marched Govind Panth; many Rájput Chiefs contributed; in Bhartpur the celebrated Suraj Mall came in with 20,000 hardy Játs.

A difference of opinion soon declared itself among these various elements. Holkar and Suraj Mall, experienced in partisan operations, pointed out to the Bháo that it was not by regular warfare that the Maráthás had heretofore baffled the armies of the Musalmáns; and they proposed that he should leave his camp and followers in some strong place, like Bhartpur or Gwalior, while he resorted to the traditional Maráthá tactics. These were to waste the country, to cut off convoys, and not to hazard fighting on a large scale till the enemy were exhausted by want or dispersed in search of forage. But the Bháo rejected these counsels with disdain, stigmatising Holkar and Suraj Mall as a couple of goatherds unfit to advise in warfare. He had seen the effect of guns and disciplined troops in southern campaigns, and he flattered himself that those advantages were now on his side rather than on that of the enemy. The guerilla experience of Holkar, the bucolic sagacity of the Ját Chief, seemed to him the timid suggestions of men ignorant of scientific war. And so the mighty host moved on to Delhi, where it arrived in December. The garrison left there was not strong enough to guard the walls; and the Bháo made his entrance without difficulty, and proceeded to surround the fortified citadel in which was situated the Imperial palace. After a brief bombardment it was taken by escalade, and a sum of seventeen *lákhs* (say £170,000) obtained for the military chest by melting down the silver with which, after so much spoliation, the ceiling of the audience-hall was still decorated.

In the meantime the Duráni Sháh was busily engaged, in his Cantonment at Anúpshahr, employed upon the organisation of the forces of Islám. All that spring he waited, with the patience of a consummate leader, and employed himself in preparing the Rohillás. Najíb was urgent that the co-operation of the Oudh Nawáb Shujá-ud-daulá should be secured at whatever cost: but he showed that the negotiation would be difficult[1]. The Lords of Irán had always shown a disposition to side with the natives against the Turanian, or immigrant, party who represented foreign conquest; and their dissidence of creed, as Shiahs, would further operate to weaken the crescentading

[1] It was believed that the Bháo, on taking possession of Delhi, had made Viswás Ráo Emperor with Shujá as Wazír.

fervour. The Sháh, perceiving the force of these arguments, begged Najíb to go to the Nawáb and persuade him to make common cause with the defenders of the faith; and in this mission the shrewd partisan was completely successful. Shujá determined on taking the plunge: he placed his family in careful custody at Lucknow, and returned with Najíb to the camp of the Sháh by whom he was warmly welcomed. Shortly after, almost before the cessation of the monsoon, the united force broke up from Anúpshahr and slowly moved, through miry ways, towards the left bank of the Jumna.

The Bháo, on this, opened negotiations with Shujá, in the hope of detaching him from his new alliance. But the prudent Najíb was ever at his convert's elbow; and, with whatever negotiations the Bháo might be amused, all the correspondence was shown to the Pathán leader[1]. The Sháh's chief minister was also consulted, and was, for his own part, not indisposed to grant terms to the Hindus. Some partition of the country seems to have been discussed; but Najíb had too much at stake to allow of his favouring any accommodation: and the only result of these negotiations was that the shaken confidence of Suraj Mall was so destroyed that he shortly after

[1] Pathán, or Rohillá, meant, in those days, much the same, viz. an Indian Afghán; but as Najíb did not belong to the confederacy of the Rohillá Province it will avoid confusion to call him a 'Pathán.' He had married a daughter of Dundi Khán, Chief of the Rohillás, but his own fief was about Sahúranpur, on the opposite side of the Ganges.

withdrew to his own country. At length arrived the *Dasahrá*, regarded in India as the termination of the monsoon and a convenient, as also an auspicious, time for the beginning of a momentous enterprise. The Bháo, accordingly, marched up the Jumna, and cut up a detached Afghán post at Kunjpurá, about eighty miles to the north of Delhi, the 20th October, 1760. The river was still brimming with autumnal floods, when the indignant Sháh threw his main army across the river to punish this act of audacity. On the afternoon of the 26th a skirmish took place at Sonpat, whence the Afgháns drove the Hindu army northward until it found shelter under the walls of Pánípat. In this position the two hosts faced each other for the next two months, during which time the wisdom of the advice tendered, the year before, by Holkar and the Ját Chief became abundantly manifest. But it was now the Maráthás who were pent up and threatened with scarcity, while the light horse of the Musalmáns wasted the country and deprived their enemies of the means of subsistence, besides cutting up detached parties: among these was Govind Panth, who was surprised while foraging, and slain with 1000 of his men, near Meerut. In an action on the 23rd December Najíb lost 3000 of his Rohillás.

At last came the $\frac{\text{6th O. S.}}{\text{17th N. S.}}$ of January 1761, when the Bháo, after a midnight council, sent off a last message to Shujá: but before he could receive an answer the Maráthás lost patience. At daybreak, having eaten their last rations, they issued from their lines, with dishevelled turbans and faces smeared with turmeric, as men devoted to death.

The Afghán army consisted of 28,000 heavy cavalry; men-in-armour mounted on big Turkmán horses. With them was an equal number of Rohillá horse, and a force of about 38,000 Hindustáni infantry —matchlockmen and pikes—while eighty heavy guns protected the position. The Hindu confederacy had suffered, by losses in skirmishing, and by desertions; but had still an immense cavalry and artillery, besides the regulars on foot. The whole number within their lines has been estimated at 300,000, but this total includes the camp-followers. The fighting men who came forth that morning probably amounted to not much more than 70,000 or, at the utmost, 80,000 good troops, with 200 guns besides a great supply of rockets (Elphinstone, p. 747). They had a multitude of light troops besides, who, however, would not count for much in a *mêlée*. They marched in an oblique line, with their left thrown forward, and guns advanced. The Bháo was in the centre, with the household troops. The extreme right consisted of cavalry under Holkar and Sindhia. The division of regular foot, under Ibráhím Gárdi, formed the left wing, with a couple of battalions bent back so as to form a half square.

On perceiving the advance the Sháh formed a similar line, of which the part consisting of Najíb and the Rohillás was on the left, opposite to Sindhia and

Holkar. The Nawáb of Oudh with 2000 cavalry came next, and then a strong body of cuirassiers under the Afghán minister Sháh Wali Khán. In the centre were the Rohillá horse under Háfiz Ráhmat and other of their chiefs. The right, composed of two Persian brigades of cavalry, faced the Gárdi. Two more divisions of cuirassiers, massed upon either wing, formed the reserve, under Afghán generals; and these were the flower of the Musalmán host. The Sháh directed the operations from the rear.

The guns of the Maráthás sent their shot over the advancing ranks of the enemy; but no sooner had the armies closed than the value of the French discipline appeared. Having defeated the attack of the Persian cavalry, Ibráhím turned upon the Rohillás with such effect that 8000 of them were quickly disposed of; and for three hours the Gárdi held the field. Shujá was paralyzed, so that he neither fled nor fought. The corps between him and Najíb was that of Sháh Wali in the centre, who had his line broken by a charge of the Bháo in person. He was dismounted, and was now in sore straits, and sent to urge Shujá to come to his support. In later wars the Nawáb was to show that he did not want for soldiership, even when engaged with the British; but this was his first experience, and he does not seem to have been equal to the occasion. Meanwhile, the sagacious Najíb had recourse to the expedient of erecting earthworks; and he was heard to say that, 'he, for one, could not afford to make any blunders.' Till noon he continued to keep off the attacks of Sindhia's horse by discharging rockets from his intrenchment. It is here that we are to picture our young adventurer, the uncle of Jankojí Sindhia, fighting by the side of his nephew, amid the roar of great guns, the whistling of musket-balls, and the low roar of the rocket-batteries, while the cries of the followers of Siva and of Vishnu crossed in the air with those of *Din! Din!* ('for the Faith') from the other side. The Sháh, from his rearward watch, saw the crisis. Bringing up his two bodies of reserved cavalry, from left and right, he charged down in support of his threatened centre. At the same moment he sent orders to his two wings to fall on the flanks of the Hindu army.

This movement began at 1 p.m.; the fight raged closely and stubbornly for more than an hour; and then the famished Hindus began to give way. The Bháo, committing his family to Holkar's protection, turned his charger's head and galloped from the field. Holkar, taking the hint, and relying on an understanding which he always maintained with the Rohillás, retired. Viswás Ráo was killed on his elephant. Among the fugitives was Janardhan Bálají, afterwards to be famous as the 'Nána Farnavis.' The rest of the battle was butchery. Forty thousand prisoners were killed on the spot. Other thousands wandered over the country till they were overtaken by the pursuing horsemen or cut up by the people of the country for the sake of their personal spoils.

Amid the rout of the fugitives young Mádhava

urged on his light Deccan mare, stimulated by the lobbing paces and roaring breath of a bony north-country horse behind him on which was mounted a gigantic Afghán trooper eager for plunder. Long was the chase, or seemed so to the anxious mind of the young Maráthá Chief: at length his mare fell at a ditch that she attempted to clear, and all hope of escape was lost. The pursuer came up; and, leaping from his horse, spat in Sindhia's face and dealt him a blow on the knee which crippled him; then stripping off his costly apparel and ornaments the Afghán rode off on the fallen man's high-bred charger, without doing any further harm.

Jankojí, the then head of the Sindhia clan, was less fortunate. Taken captive in the lost battle he was slain next day with a multitude of other captives, in spite of earnest efforts made in his behalf by the Oudh Wazír. A headless body, found some miles from the field, was believed to be all that remained of the once splendid and powerful Sheodásheo Bháo; and the honours of the Hindu cremation were accordingly paid to those remains at the prayer of the same nobleman, Shujá-ud-daulá, whose Indian sympathies have been already noticed. The gallant Ibráhím Gárdi was also taken, covered with wounds: the Afghán leaders reproached him bitterly for serving the heathen against his co-religionists; and he died a few days later, his injuries being neglected or, as was believed by some, purposely maltreated. In all these matters the Shia Nawáb, Shujá-ud-daulá was not by any means satisfied with the attention paid to him by the Sháh who, for his part, set but little value on the Nawáb's assistance. After events were to show that Shujá was no mean soldier; but in the present campaign his co-operation certainly appears to have been somewhat lukewarm. He now departed, without showing or receiving any extraordinary tokens of respect or friendship; and he never again took part in religious warfare.

The Sháh soon after returned to his own country: but before doing so he proclaimed the absent Sháh 'Alam, appointing a provisional government to act at Delhi, at the head of which was Mírzá Jawan Bakht, eldest son of Sháh 'Alam; Najíb Khán, with the title of Najíb-ud-daulá, was to be chief minister, for war and peace, as before the campaign.

The campaign of 1760–1 is an instance, in the first place, of the value of generalship and firmness. Like his ally, Najíb, the Afghán Sháh, 'could not afford to make any mistakes.' The Bháo, on the contrary, however valiant, was arrogant and careless. In its military and political incidents also, it will be found in many respects deserving of attention. It is not only an exemplary instance of the height to which the power of the southern confederacy had grown, but it is the first occasion of an Asiatic power using the new resources of scientific warfare against mediaeval methods. The latter, it is true, prevailed; in spite of the employment of artillery and regular infantry the enemy won the victory by reiterated charges of mailed men-at-arms. Yet, for all that, the behaviour of the Gárdis, imperfectly trained and without European officers as they were, was sufficiently remarkable to have afforded instruction to such a mind as the youthful Sindhia's. On his own future fortunes the campaign was destined, as we shall presently see, to exercise a still more direct influence. By the temporary depression of their confederacy it deterred the Maráthás from an attack upon Bengal in which they would probably have been joined by Shujá and Sháh 'Alam, and would perhaps have succeeded in extirpating the still slender and struggling power of the British Company. Had they been successful in Bengal there would have been nothing to arrest the Maráthás in Northern India. Whatever wars might have awaited them in the South, there would have been no opening for the peculiar ambition of Mádhava Sindhia; he might have distinguished himself against Haidar or the Nizám: but he would never have had the opportunity of coming to an understanding with Warren Hastings, or of making himself master of the Mughal Empire in Hindustán.

It is for these reasons that the circumstances of the attack on Northern India by the Poona Government and its bloody repulse by the Afgháns are of so much moment, occurring when they did. At no later period, indeed, would the campaign have been of the same importance. In a few years after the rout of Pánípat the Sikh power had become consolidated. Never again were the Afgháns to have their own way in the Punjab. A few more raids and incursions were to take place, each less successful than its predecessor; and then the new semi-Hindu confederacy of the Sikhs, the famous Khálsa, was to settle down, like a wall of concrete, a dam against the encroachment of the Northern flood. And not only so, but the formation of the Khálsa wall not only kept out the tide of invasion, but it produced a still more unexpected and, even yet, little-noticed change. From the middle of the sixteenth century there had been a constant immigration of individual adventures from Turkestán and Persia, which had furnished the Mughal Empire with great philosophers, beautiful princesses, brave generals, and able politicians and statesmen. This system of more peaceful invasion also was now to cease. After the half-dozen Mughal Chiefs now in the country had passed away there were to be no more of those powerful individualities to lead the more pliable characters of Hindustán and shape the fortunes of the people.

For the present, Najíb-ud-daulá, one of the last of these immigrants, was supreme at Delhi. Of the Hindu hosts who had entered the capital eighteen months ago, hardly a fragment was left to struggle home to the Deccan. Hindustán was saved, but so as by fire, delivered, but quite demoralised. Of the condition of the harassed inhabitants we may form some notion from the language of a native writer quoted by the historian of Rájputána.

'The people of Hindustán, at this period, thought only of personal safety and gratification. Misery was disregarded by those who escaped it: and man, centred solely in self, felt not for his kind. This selfishness, destructive of virtue both public and private, became universal in Hindustán after the invasion of Nádir Sháh; nor have the people become more virtuous since, and consequently are neither more happy nor more independent' (Tod's *Rajasthan*).

Meanwhile the Maráthá confederacy had sustained a shock which was likely to deter its members from again disturbing the peace of Hindustán for some time to come. With the losses in preliminary engagements, the slaughter on the field, and the subsequent massacres of prisoners by the Afgháns and of fugitives by the peasantry of the surrounding villages, it was estimated that three-fourths of the grand army had disappeared: according to Grant Duff 'nearly two hundred thousand Maráthás perished in the campaign.'

An effort had been made to save them and secure success. During the nine or ten weeks for which the Bháo had been blockaded at Pánípat reports of his condition had reached his cousin at Poona. The Peshwá was a voluptuary, but not destitute of spirit: and he seems to have done his best to succour his kinsman and his son. In December he set out from Ahmadnagar, with such forces as he had been able to collect: and he had reached the Narbadá when he was accosted, on his march across that stream, by a messenger sent express by a banker attached to the army, hurrying with news to the banker's correspondents in the Deccan. Tearing open the letter carried by this man the Peshwá read the ominous words: 'Two pearls have been melted; twenty-seven gold *mohrs* have been lost: of silver and copper the totals cannot be cast up.' In this figurative language, employed for prudential reasons, the Peshwá discovered a too true description of the ruin that had overtaken his officers and men.

Presently the scattered fugitives began to trickle into the camp, and to confirm the terrible tidings. Grief and despair took possession of high and low. Sadly the Peshwá gave orders for the homeward march of the now useless reinforcements: his health of mind and body, already shaken by his self-indulgent habits, rapidly gave way: in June, 1761, he died at Poona of 'a broken heart.' He was succeeded in the Presidency of the Maráthá States by his second son, Mádhava Ráo, the namesake of Sindhia.

In the following pages we shall try to unfold the character and conduct of the great man who, thus nursed in foraying, disaster, and anarchy, and exposed for the greater part of his life to all sorts of hostile attacks and intrigues, was to make a successful inroad on this state of unlaw, and to restore the beginnings of prosperity to an afflicted people.

It has been mentioned that Mádhava was an illegitimate son of the deceased Patel and slipper-bearer, Ránojí Sindhia. The family of Ránojí is believed to have been of noble origin, a younger branch of one which held the Chieftainship of Kanerkhair, some sixteen miles from Sátára, and who had held a *mansab*, or military peerage, under the Mughal Empire. But the father of Ránojí had fallen upon evil days: he had become a *Patel*, or village manager, and his son had been fain to take service as a private trooper in the *Pagah*, or body-guard, of the Peshwá Bálají Viswanáth. Employed to take care of the slippers of his master during any interview that the latter might have with the Rájá, it was Ránojí's duty to present them when the Peshwá came out again. On one occasion of this kind the interview was long, and the Patel weary, so that he fell asleep at his post: but the Peshwá on emerging from the Presence was struck by finding that, even in his sleep, the faithful attendant had hold of the shoes in both hands, with which he clasped them to his breast. From that moment the Patel's fortune was made, and he became an officer of rank with a *Jaigir*, or military fief, in Northern Málwá, where he fixed his head-quarters at the famous old Hindu town of Ujjain, the capital of the legendary Vikramáditya. This province, as already mentioned, had been formerly held by Ásaf Jáh, the founder of the existing dynasty of Haidarábád; when he went to conquer the Deccan in 1721 the province passed from one official to the other until, in the decrepitude of the Empire, an attempt was made to produce a valid viceroy in the person of Jai Singh II, the loyal and learned Dhiráj of Jaipur.

About the middle of the century Bálají Bájí Ráo, the third Peshwá, whose defeat and death have been just described, finally obtained possession, under the pretence of holding it as a vassal of the now moribund Empire. But the Peshwá was too busy with other affairs, more remote and more important: so he presently proceeded to parcel out his newly acquired territory, granting the southern portion to Malhár Ji Holkar, and the northern to Ránojí Sindhia.

Ránojí, the original Patel and shoe-bearer, had fixed his capital, as we have seen, in Northern Málwá, where he died (at some undetermined period) leaving five sons: Mádhava, the subject of our memoir, being illegitimate, and the youngest but one. All his brothers died before Pánípat or in that action; so that, by the time we have reached, the maimed fugitive left to die on the wayside by his Afghán pursuer was the last of his race. The family, however, was saved from extinction by the opportune arrival of a Musalmán water-carrier driving a bullock on whose back was the *pakál*, or ox-skin, used for transporting water. This man whose name was Rāná Khán, lifted the wounded Chief to the back of the bullock and conveyed him to a place of safety: for which piece of humanity he ultimately received a munificent reward. The young Sindhia, who never forgot either a benefit or a wrong, always called the Musalmán waterman his 'brother'; and, on the latter entering the military service, watched his career to such purpose that Ráná Khán rose to be a general officer and commanded armies in several subsequent actions of importance.

At the time of these tragic events, Mádhava Ráo was about thirty years of age; but the fact that he was not born in wedlock has operated to keep the exact date and place of his birth uncertain. Being now the only capable representative of the clan, he obtained, though not without some difficulty, the succession to his father's fiefs and the command which was involved in their possession. The old school of officials opposed him on account of his illegitimacy; and it is said that this circumstance caused him to conceive a prejudice against his own countrymen and to show a strong preference for foreigners when he came to construct a civil and military administration. He displayed symptoms of insubordination, too; and ran a great risk of punishment for lingering at Poona when ordered to join the army after the death of his old comrade Holkar: the circumstances, however, were not altogether discreditable to Sindhia.

Malhárji Holkar, who was originally a shepherd, had distinguished himself in the wars that led to the occupation of Málwá. After the battle of Pánípat, in 1761, he returned to Málwá, and died there about four years after, leaving his fief to be administered by Ahalya Bái, the widow of his son and guardian of his infant grandson, of whom she was the mother. This lady, of whose remarkable talents and virtues we shall speak more fully hereafter, selected as her residence the pleasant village of Indore, where she began building in 1770, and which is now a populous city, and the capital of the Holkar State. Before that period there had been several other chief towns, at various times; such as Kampil, Sárangpur, and Mándu, all of which have long since fallen into decay.

The grandson of Malhárji did not long survive him; and the Poona Regent, Rughnáth Ráo—known in English histories as 'Ragoba'—called on the dowager to adopt a male heir to the State and property of the House of Holkar. But the lady refused, declaring that she would carry on the administration herself. On this Rughnáth, who wielded provisional power at Poona, threatened to make an armed attack upon the widow and daughter-in-law of his feudatory with the object of plundering her property and destroying the power of the House. But Mádhava refused to act against the family of his deceased comrade; and since he held a principal command, and since the Bhonsla of Nágpur joined in his opposition, the Regent was obliged to desist from the nefarious enterprise.

The route of the army collected by the Regent was accordingly diverted. Placed under the nominal command of the Quarter-Master-General, one Visáji Krishn, the expedition was henceforth directed against the meagre dominions of Delhi, then under the protection of Najíb-ud-daulá. But Sindhia was not the man to draw chestnuts out of the fire for others. He was already laying the foundation of sovereignty in Central India, where his fief was; and, being in command of a choice body of 15,000 cavalry, he soon made himself virtual master of the territories between the Narbadá and the Chambal.

In 1769, however, he joined his forces to those of the Quarter-Master-General, and aided in a systematic plunder of the Játs of Bhartpur. This is not the place for a detailed account of that remarkable race which has long inhabited the land of the Hindus; among them but scarcely of them, industrious in peace, tenacious in war, and maintaining their peculiar tribal customs. They first made their appearance in the Indus valley, whence they spread westward by the time of Tamerlane, who records that they were Musalmáns in name but unequalled robbers by nature. In the reign of 'Alamgír they had got as far as Agra and Bhartpur, and in the Punjab had amalgamated with the Khattrís to form the Sikh community. In 1684 and again in 1691 expeditions were sent against them by the Imperial Government, in opposing which they chose one Chúráman, the lord of Sánsani, as their leader, who was killed in battle in 1720. Chúráman's grandson was Suraj Mall, whom we saw advising the Bháo in 1760 and saving himself from the ruin that he foresaw. With the aid of these sturdy yeomen Najíb for some time made head against the Maráthá general's attacks; especially in 1765, when another column of the Maráthá army was at the same time driven out of the country of Cawnpur by Colonel Carnac. But the Játs were never famous for their generosity; and no sooner were the Maráthás expelled than they thought the opportunity good for taking their share in the pickings of the carcase. Suraj Mall had obtained possession of the imperial city of Agra with its great fortified palace; he also took several strong places in the Mewát Hills S.W. of Delhi and was threatening the valley of the Upper Jumna. At this time he had engaged the services of Sombre (Walter Reinhardt) the famous condottiere, with a battalion of trained Sepoys, a detail of artillery and about three hundred Europeans of various nationalities. But the Ulysses of Delhi was a match for the Autolycus of Bhartpur; the Ját Chief was killed, and his men were beaten back into the Bhartpur country before the end of 1765. They next attacked the Jaipur Rájputs; and, being again worsted, were deserted by Sombre who never remained long with a falling cause. A period of confusion in the Ját State followed; but the youngest son of Suraj Mall at last became Rájá, or Thákur as they called him; and under him the Ját power still extended from Agra to Alwar, with a revenue of two millions sterling and an army of 60,000 men.

Early in 1767 the Sikhs threatened Najíb, but this only brought down the Afgháns, who overran the Punjab under Ahmad Sháh. The Sháh halted for some time on the scene of his former victory at Pánípat, where he confirmed former arrangements, and returned thence to his own country. Soon after his departure the Maráthá army crossed the Chambal, advanced through the Jaipur plains which they wasted, and made the attack on Bhartpur already mentioned. Having rendered the Játs submissive they proceeded to threaten Delhi in 1769 and opened negotiations with Najíb; the immediate object being that the Maráthás might, without molestation from the Musalmáns, collect *chaut* (as their phrase went)[1] in the territories between the Chambal, which was Sindhia's boundary, and the Jumna which then practically marked off the land remaining under the direct rule, or influence, of the Court of Delhi.

The army which finally crossed the Narbadá in 1769, under the Quarter-Master-General, was reviewed in Málwá, after the junction of Sindhia's troops and those of the Indore dowager under her able general Takújí Holkar. Each of these Chiefs was the leader of fifteen thousand horse, while the Quarter-Master himself commanded twenty thousand more, inclusive of the light marauding cavalry so disastrously known in later years as 'Pindárís.' There was also a large body of infantry with guns; but the men of those arms were not Maráthás. Some were natives of Málwá, others Hindus from the Doáb: the most valued and trusted of all being Arabs, and Abyssinians, and seafaring men from the Conean and the Malabar coast.

With the exception of the short raid by the followers of Holkar in 1764–5, this was the first appearance of a Maráthá army in Hindustán since the disaster of Pánípat. In the interval many things

[1] *Chaut* = 25 per cent., from a word meaning 'one-fourth.'

had happened, including the deposition and expulsion of Mír Kásim from the Eastern Súbas, and the establishment of the British Company's servants there in the capacity of civil administrators under Imperial patent. The fugitive Emperor had been enthroned under the joint protection of the British and the Nawáb Wazír; and now held faded state in the halls of his ancestors at Allahábád; so fallen that he had to discontinue the music of his palace band on the remonstrance of the British commandant, whose repose was disturbed by the barbaric strains of which an awe-struck European visitor had once declared that he found in them 'something majestical' (Bernier). Weary of these restraints Sháh 'Alam was more than ever yearning for a restoration to Delhi; and, without taking his British patrons into the smallest confidence, he had opened negotiations with the leaders of the Maráthás which perhaps involved the ultimate and real object of their reappearance in Hindustán, where they respected the palace and the person of the Prince-Regent.

We are now to enter on a most embroiled and confusing period, of intrigue and of war; in which considerable demands must, of necessity, be made upon the attention of the most patient reader. The only excuse that can be offered is that the period is one which, while it marks the gradual pacification of Hindustan, displays the penetration of the great Englishman who founded the Indian Empire without conquest and without unnecessary bloodshed.

CHAPTER III

From the Restoration of the Emperor to the Peace of Salbái

The negotiations opened by the Quarter-Master-General were conducted by Takújí, the officer who had, as we have already seen, been selected by the widowed daughter-in-law of the son of the deceased Chief, Malhár Ráo, to carry on the affairs of the Holkar clan. Though not a member of the late Chief's family by blood, Takújí assumed the traditionary policy of the House, a portion of which was alliance with the Patháns or native Musalmáns, of whom the Rohillás were now the most actively conspicuous. Mádhava, on the other hand, was both opposed to that class by hereditary impulse and because he perceived that in Najíb, supported by the Patháns, he had the most formidable rival in his ulterior designs. It would be idle to compare the two men who now divided the diplomatic direction of Maráthá affairs as they also did the government of Málwá. The leader of the Holkar clan, who held possession of the southern portion of the province resting on the range of the Vindhya north of the Narbadá, was a good officer and a faithful subordinate to the strong-willed woman who had raised him from obscurity: to him it was sufficient that the immediate interests of his mistress, and of the Maráthá confederacy at large, should be duly provided for. It was deemed advisable, in that view, to profit by the tendered friendship of Najíb, who had conquered the Játs and might at any time renew the league of Islám: he had been the mainspring of the combination of 1760, and he was an evident favourite of the Afghán Sháh to whom he had then been so useful. Najíb was invited to visit the Maráthá camp, which he did; but he was worn out and knew that he had not long to live. He placed the hand of his son in that of Takúji, whose protection he requested, as if he foresaw how much that weak and worthless creature would need friends. He also attempted to conciliate Sindhia, but here he entirely failed. 'I require revenge,' the latter Chief said, 'for so much desolation and so many deaths, for the blood of my brothers and my nephews and my own perpetual mutilation; nor am I satisfied because my friend chooses to make this Musalmán noble his brother. Nevertheless, I am the Peshwá's servant; and if he sanctions such an alliance my part is to obey.'

In holding this language, which is recorded by a contemporary writer, Sindhia struck the notes which were the dominant and the subdominant of his tune from first to last; the preservation of the Maráthá confederacy and the observation of his own schemes and interests.

Najíb left the Maráthá camp after making these arrangements and retired to Najíbábád, a town that he had founded on the eastern side of the Ganges, and there he died, in October 1770, leaving his estates, and his post at Delhi, to Zábita Khán, the son already mentioned. The character of Najíb was eulogised during his lifetime by Mr. Vansittart, President of the British Settlement in Bengal, who recorded his opinion that Najíb-ud-daulá was 'the only example in Hindustán of a character at once good and great.'

In 1770 the Rohillá power was declining; the districts which Dundi Khán had acquired in the Doáb he had been compelled to surrender to the Maráthás; and on his death he had left the province of Katahr, the present Rohilkhand, in the hands of a loose federation of Pathán Chiefs under the Protectorate of Háfiz Ráhmat Khán. Their expulsion from the Doáb had been effected by Mádhava, who was also charged with the repression of the Játs.

Meanwhile Zábita Khán was already beginning to show the fickle falseness of character which marked the rest of his brief and inglorious career. While the Maráthás were levying contributions in Rájputána, the Ját country, the Upper Doáb and Rohilkhand, he made no attempt to conciliate them or to make friends in other quarters; but contented himself with keeping back the revenues due to the absent Emperor and violating the sanctity of the Delhi palace, that last retreat of the great House of Timúr, by intrigues with princesses of the imperial family. In the beginning of 1771, the palace was occupied by the Maráthá Chiefs before whom Zábita fled, retiring to his northern possessions, whence he began negotiating with Takúji Holkar who was contemplating the early restoration of the Emperor Sháh 'Alam.

That vagrant monarch had, as previously stated, been pensioned by Clive after the defeat of the Nawáb Shujá in 1765. Since that time he had continued to reside, under British protection, at Allahábád with direct administrative jurisdiction over the adjoining districts on the N.W. But he had never ceased to dream of a return to Delhi and a revival of the Empire of his fathers; for the realisation of which dream he now seemed to see a favourable opening in the death of Najíb. The leading men at Delhi, too, were very weary of the Patháns, and anticipated from the restoration of the Mughal monarchy a relief from Rohillá licence, and perhaps a renewed chance of employment in public affairs. The Nawáb of Oudh, on the other hand, was by no means in favour of the scheme; while the British authorities, when it was communicated to them openly, expressed their strong disapproval.

In these circumstances Takúji opened negotiations with the Sháh, or the Sháh with him, through the mediation of a loose Mughal lord, known only by his title of Hissám-ud-daulá and by the reputation that has survived him of having been the Sháh's agent in less respectable procuration. There is no record of Sindhia's share in the transaction: the only certain detail that we know is that the Sháh promised to pay ten *lákhs* (say £100,000) as a present fee to the Poona darbár; while the cession of the districts which he had received from the Nawáb under British influence also probably formed part of the consideration, implied if not expressed.

Accordingly, disregarding the advice of the British Government and the dissuasions of the Nawáb Shujá, Sháh 'Alam advanced up the Doáb, arriving before the end of the monsoon at Farukhábád on the frontier of Rohilkhaṇd. The main body of the Maráthá army of Hindustán kept order at Delhi and awaited the Sháh's arrival; but Sindhia, ever active in forwarding his own great design, marched out with a chosen force, joined his Majesty in his camp, and escorted him to the capital, which he entered on the 25th December, 1771. For the next few months Sindhia and the rest of the Maráthá leaders remained in and about the metropolis, engaged in measures of defence against Zábita Khán, who was living at the head of the Doáb. Here he had several strong places, such as Ghausgarh, Sahāranpur, and Sakartál—where the Ganges, after emerging from the hills, first becomes capable of navigation. He had ceased for the time to profit by the protection of Holkar and was engaged in stirring up his kindred on the other side of the river, the Patháns of Rohilkhand. In that province Zábita had a fourth strong-hold, Najíbábád, already mentioned as the place of his father's death, the citadel of which was called Pathargarh (the 'Stone Fortress'). Hither he retired on hearing of the projected hostilities, so that he might have the river on his front, and on his rear the friendly country of the Rohillás. But the latter were at once neutralised by the action of Shujá-ud-daulá, the Nawáb of Oudh, whose readiness to co-operate with the supposed projects of the Emperor was quickened by views which he himself was maturing. In all that was being planned at Delhi it was the vindictiveness of the Maráthás, directed by Sindhia, that was really at work; nevertheless, a restored emperor must be supposed to have some voice in imperial politics. Moreover, whatever may have been his own feelings in the matter, Sháh 'Alam had a minister, for peace and for war, who was certainly capable of both making and executing enterprises of great pith and moment. This was Mírzá Najaf Khán, a Persian immigrant of high lineage and distinguished ability, the last great type of the class who, before the Sikhs were strong enough to bar the road through the Punjab, had been finding careers in India ever since the days of Akbar.

Headed ostensibly by the Sháh, who made some marches with the army, the Maráthás marched out of Delhi in 1771, accompanied by a small but well-appointed imperial force, consisting of the body-guard of cadet cavaliers (*Ahdis* as they were called[1]) and the 'Red battalion,' a body of regular infantry under a French officer named Médoc. The passage of the

[1] *v. sup.* p. 25.

Ganges was easily effected; for at that time of year, before the snows on the Himálayas have begun to melt, the Ganges was fordable at almost all points of its upper course; and the Rohillás were deceived into believing that Sindhia and Holkar meant to cross at a point higher up the stream, where the usual crossing was at other seasons. Paralyzed by the menacing attitude of Shujá, the Rohillás withheld their support: and Zábita hurriedly evacuated Pathargarh, leaving his family and the treasure which his father had accumulated during ten years of office. His son, Ghulám Kádir was mutilated and converted into a Zanána-page in retaliation for the liberties taken in the palace after Najíb's death; it seemed as if Sindhia's revenge was beginning.

But the fall of the Rohillás was delayed by dissensions among their foes. The Emperor, who had been treated with but little respect by the Maráthás, retired to Delhi; and the latter proceeded to admit the fugitive Zábita to pardon, and restored the captives taken at Pathargarh for a moderate indemnity in cash. They then advanced upon Agra where they passed the rainy season, while the Rohillás opened a negotiation with the Nawáb of Oudh, whose designs they had not penetrated, and with whose alliance they hoped to reconstruct the Muhammadan league which had been, temporarily, so successful in 1760. By the good offices of the British Government of Bengal a treaty was concluded by virtue whereof the Protector of Rohilkhand bound himself and his brethren to give their support to the Musalmán cause and to pay the Nawáb forty *lákhs* (say £400,000) in four instalments on condition of the Maráthás being excluded from their province. This treaty, which proved the ruin of the Rohillás, was concluded on the 11th July, 1772. The following extract contains the essential clause:—

'The Vazir' [Shujá's titular rank] 'shall establish the Rohelas obliging the Maráthás to retire, either peacefully or by war. If at any time they shall again enter the country their expulsion is the business of the Vazir. The Rohela Sirdárs, in pursuance of the above, do agree to pay to the Vazir the sum of forty *lákhs* of rupis,' &c. &c.

Violent dissensions among the Rohillás ensued, and the province became the scene of terrible confusion and anarchy. At the same time Zábita, untrue to the league of his co-religionists, was making secret terms with the Maráthás; he for his part seeking to be replaced in the conduct of Delhi affairs, in which the titular Wazír took no active part; while the Maráthás, stimulated by Sindhia, were preparing for another struggle with the Musalmáns. The virtues and abilities of Mírzá Najaf were already attracting attention; and Zábita, in plotting against the Muhammadan league, was also contriving the ruin of a formidable rival.

The new allies conceived that their purposes would be advanced by stirring up trouble in the vicinity of Delhi, so as to bring the Mírzá into disgrace and alarm, the Emperor into seeking their aid. With this view they instigated the Thákur of the Játs, Ranjít

Singh, to renew certain claims upon the districts on the right bank of the Jumna, just above the capital. In pursuance of these claims the Ját forces moved against the fort of Ballabgarh, then held by a Balúch Chieftain whom, as a Musalmán feudatory, the Mírzá felt bound to support. A Mughal force was therefore sent from Delhi to check the Játs; the Maráthás moved up in support of the latter; and then the Mírzá himself repaired to the scene, taking with him M. Médoc's regular infantry.

All these movements and intrigues disgusted Sindhia, who had no desire that the son of Najíb-ud-daulá should prosper, or that the Empire should receive its *coup-de-grâce* before he should be in a position to use its imposing remains for his own objects. He therefore withdrew with his fine force to Rájputána, where he provided the subsistence of his men by living at free quarters in the country of the Rájá of Jaipur.

In the meantime Holkar threw himself between the Ját army and the Mírzá, whom he encountered at Badrpur, about ten miles S. of Delhi. After four days of obstinate fighting, in which discipline vainly contended against numbers, the Mírzá was overwhelmed and driven back upon the capital which both the combatant parties entered together. Holkar was admitted into the palace by Hissám-ud-daulá, and the objects of temporary league were obtained. Mírzá Najaf was directed to withdraw, and his office of *Amir-ul-amra* ('Premier') was transferred to

Zábita, while the Emperor made, or confirmed, the grant of the Lower Doáb to the Maráthás. These events occurred in December 1772, just a twelvemonth after the Restoration. Hardly were they concluded when news arrived from Poona which disturbed all plans. The young Peshwá had not exercised independent authority more than seven years when he died, probably from the effects of a disorder from which he had long suffered, on the 18th November. The Regency was resumed by his uncle, Rughnáth Ráo, or, as the British called him, 'Ragoba,' who was known to aspire to the actual Peshwáship. An era of conflict, perhaps of civil war, was felt to be at hand: the first thought of the Quarter-Master-General and the other Chiefs was to reach Poona and be ready to take a hand in any eventualities. Indeed the new Peshwá himself issued the order for their recall, feeling that he might need the support of the army against the ambitious machinations of his uncle.

Before either Sindhia or Holkar, however, made their way to the capital other developments were taking shape. On 30th August, 1773, the new Peshwá had followed his brother to the funeral pyre, assassinated, as was supposed, by the aspiring Raghuba, who assumed the title and office of Peshwá and commenced hostilities against the Musalmán Chiefs of the south, Haidar and the Nizám. But, before he could derive the advantage he hoped for from these gratuitous attacks upon his neighbours, he was recalled to Poona by tidings of an event which threatened all his ambitious projects. The party opposed to him had already taken the precaution of removing the late Peshwá's pregnant widow to the security of a mountain fastness, where she was now safely delivered of a boy. This infant was at once proclaimed Peshwá by the ministers at Poona; and being attacked by Raghuba, they inflicted on him a crushing defeat under the walls of that city. Raghuba fled north to meet the returning army, and arrived at Indore just as Sindhia and Holkar, the two Chiefs of Málwá, had pitched their camp there. Both Chiefs promised him their support; and they then turned aside into Gujarát, with Raghuba, in order to secure for him the support of the Gáekwár who ruled that province. Their next measure, suggested probably by Sindhia, was to seek an alliance with the British authorities at Bombay, then a very minor factory on one of the islands of the archipelago on the Konkan coast supposed to have been the *Heptanesia* of Arrian. The Company's servants there had long desired to round off the possessions of their employers by the acquisition of the old Portuguese harbour of Bassein and of the extensive island of Salsette which barred their own port; and they now, without consulting the Governor-General, promised to furnish Raghuba with British troops on condition of his obtaining these coveted places and paying for the support of the contingent. So eager, indeed, were the members of the Bombay Council that they lent Raghuba a force of 1500 sepoys without obtaining his formal consent to the equivalent cession. The places in question, moreover, were on fair grounds claimed by the Portuguese; and, as soon as the nature of the negotiations became known at Goa, the Viceroy there began to set on foot an expedition for their recovery. Upon hearing of this Governor Hornby, without further ado, took summary possession both of Salsette and of Bassein.

As we are not tracing the history of British India it will not be necessary that the reader should be troubled with detailed comments on these proceedings: it will be enough to observe that they were hasty and ill-conceived. Nevertheless, had Mr. Hornby secured the sanction and support of the Supreme Government, to which recent parliamentary enactment had rendered him subordinate, and had his audacity been seconded by due courage and ability among his military officers, Raghuba might have been installed as Peshwá, and much of the history of Mádhava Ráo Sindhia and of Hindustán might have been different from what it was.

But, before any active measures could be taken by Raghuba and his supporters, the Poona Regency had been at work upon some of the latter. Holkar's patroness, the daughter-in-law of the late Malhár Ráo, was a lady of singular ability and virtue, whose sympathies were easily gained for the other widow and the innocent child of her late sovereign. Sindhia, also, who at this period usually acted with the Holkar clan who were his partners in Málwá, withdrew from the cause of the usurper. Raghuba was once more defeated, and he fled to the camp of Colonel Keating at Surat with a slender following, in December, 1774.

The consequence was a fresh treaty between Raghuba and the Bombay factory, still without the sanction of the Supreme Government, by which the occupation of Salsette and Bassein was confirmed with territory yielding a large revenue, in consideration whereof, and of a large present payment, the British contingent was to be doubled in strength. Keating was reinforced and ordered to march on Poona in order to instal Raghuba by force of arms; and the Regency promptly ordered out all their available forces to repulse the movement. The armies manœuvred about Surat; and, in spite of an almost overwhelming superiority of numbers, the host of the darbár of Regency was finally encountered by Keating. His own force was but small, and the troops of Raghuba hampered rather than assisted their operations. In very difficult ground, at a place called Áras near the head of the gulf of Cambay, Keating fought a severe action in which he lost two hundred and twenty-two men, among them seven European officers, and only defeated the enemy at last by his own intrepidity and the good behaviour of his small British contingent. This was on the 18th May, 1775. In the evening of the 10th June he overtook them at Bhaopir, near Broach: but again the troops of Raghuba encumbered his attack; and the army of the Regency escaped during the night, throwing their guns into the Narbadá lest their flight should be impeded.

These things, we may be sure, did not escape the notice of Sindhia. That shrewd observer was never slow to learn a lesson, whether in politics or in war; and the course of his conduct might have been at once determined by what he then learned of the value of discipline and military conduct, as displayed by the British, had not their political vacillations, due to causes then beyond his ken, introduced a disturbing influence. Not that Warren Hastings by any means approved of the doings of the Bombay Government; but he felt that they had compromised British credit. He had to accept an accomplished fact. If you kept the ceded districts, and no one proposed their surrender except the ministry at Poona, you were bound to fulfil the terms on which they had been obtained. But, here again, he was in a minority. Francis and his colleagues, whose resolutions Hastings had no power to reverse, were determined to do the things that they ought not to have done while omitting to do the things that they ought to have done. So Colonel Upton was sent to Poona, as a special Envoy from the Government of Bengal, made supreme by the Regulating Act of 1773, and his orders were to disavow the proceedings of the Bombay Council, and to open negotiations with the defeated Regency. Mistaking Upton's moderation of manner for weakness, the Regency took at first high and menacing ground. But when the Bengal Council became informed that the terms proposed included not only the surrender of Raghuba but the restoration of the ceded territory, that body rejected the claims. Eventually a compromise ensued, certain articles being agreed to between Colonel Upton, of the one part, and Sukh Rám Bápu and his colleagues, of the other, which were embodied in the Treaty of Purandhar. Raghuba was to be abandoned, if not actually given up, his army being disbanded. Salsette was to be retained, so long as the Governor-General might think proper; the rents of Broach and the surrounding district were to be given up by the darbár, with a war indemnity of twelve *lákhs* of rupees.

Neither the Bombay Council nor its *protégé* was disposed to submit to these conditions. The ministers at Poona soon found that their diplomatic successes were more apparent than real. The moving spirit there was the old Bráhman, Pandit Sukh Rám Bápu, a cautious but resolute man, who had been supported in these affairs by a young rival who was beginning to push himself to the front. This man, also a Bráhman, was named Bálají Janardhan, better known by his official title of 'Nána Farnavis' (v. p. 43). For purposes of his own the Nána had acted with Pandit Sukh Rám: and being in secret the paramour of Gangá Bai, mother of the young Peshwá, he was necessarily a valuable ally. It was one of Sindhia's constant objects to act as umpire between opposing parties in the Poona darbár; but, now that opposition was for the moment ended, he was naturally driven into general hostility, the more so as he had an old-standing grudge against Sukh Rám who had never been his friend.

While Poona politics were in this condition Raghuba's conduct gave rise to fresh complications. Repudiating the Treaty of Purandhar to which he had, of course, been no party, he peremptorily declined to disband his troops and repaired to the British station of Surat, where he was welcomed and harboured by the Bombay Government. Colonel Upton vainly protested against what he deemed an infraction of the treaty: Raghuba appealed to the Court of Directors; and Warren Hastings supported the appeal. Orders eventually came out from London, in virtue of which the articles of the treaty were tacitly abrogated, and Raghuba was invited to Bombay, where he was received with honour and granted a monthly stipend of ten thousand rupees (November, 1776).

Affairs at Poona became more and more complicated. Early in 1777 a French adventurer, named St. Lubin, landed on the coast and represented himself to the ministers at Poona as an ambassador from the Court of Versailles. Elated by this unexpected alliance, the Nána began to give offence to his colleagues. Sukh Rám took alarm and joined with other powerful personages in a scheme for the restoration of Raghuba, with which object negotiations were opened with the Bombay Government. As Takújí Holkar espoused the quarrel and lent the aid of his troops, the Nána, who was not by nature a fighting man, judged it prudent to retire; and the Bombay Council, with the approval of the Supreme Government, which sent a force under Colonel Leslie to operate in support, declared the intention of restoring Raghuba by force of arms.

In this conjunction of events Sindhia recovered his favourite position of umpire. He was at no time perhaps, certainly not at this time, on terms of personal hostility towards the Nána. Towards Sukh Rám, on the other hand, he was never friendly. With Takúji Holkar he had many ties of comradeship and old association. He at once threw all his power and influence into the Nána's side of the scales. Accompanied by the famous Hari Panth, and having detached Holkar from the side of Sukh Rám, he marched upon Purandhar, and restored the Nána to office, on the 8th June, 1778.

Still, things were far from looking bad for Raghuba's cause; under orders from home, it was warmly espoused by both the Governments of Bombay and Bengal. Undaunted by the restoration to power of the Nána Farnavis, unmindful of the Treaty of Purandhar and of the fact that they had no right to interfere since St. Lubin had been dismissed from Poona and had left India, and without awaiting the arrival of the still distant Bengal column, the Bombay authorities resolved to attack the Regency without delay. Assembling a force of 4000 men, of whom a fourth part consisted of British troops, they gave the command to a valetudinarian of ripe years but raw experience, named Egerton. To ensure their views being enforced they associated with him a member of their own body, General Carnac, who had left Bengal with a not too brilliant record. Professing the utmost need for haste they allowed three months to go by in preparation and in marches of two miles a day. On the other side Sindhia, having effected a reconciliation between old Sukh Rám and the Nána, assembled a strong force on the top of the Ghâts. On the 9th January the British force arrived at Talegáon, twenty miles from Poona: but it got no farther. The commanding officer fell sick, the military Member of Council lost his head; the column was hemmed in and cowed into retreat; officers and men became demoralised; the stores were burned, the guns thrown into a pond: it was mainly due to the courage and conduct of one officer, Captain Hartley, that the troops were enabled to reach Wadgáon, just three miles to the rear. By the 13th the little column had lost three hundred and fifty-two of the original number, including no less than fifteen European officers. A convention became necessary, a condition of which was the extradition of the Pretender; but Raghuba saved the British officers this great degradation by voluntary agreement with Sindhia, to whom he ultimately surrendered. When the British agent urged that he had no power to treat for the surrender of territory, Sindhia replied by a rapid thrust of debating dexterity. 'Show us, then,' he replied, 'the authority by which you have broken the Treaty of Purandhar.'

Sindhia was urbane and clement, but exacted the fullest surrender possible. The advance of the Bengal column was to be instantly countermanded: for himself personally he insisted on the cession of Broach with a gift of forty-one thousand rupees as gratuities to his followers.

This disgraceful affair led to unexpected results. The officers who had caused the disaster and signed the convention were dismissed the service; the Bengal column pursued its march towards Central India; strangest of all, Sindhia began to hesitate in the scheme, to which he had hitherto shown favour, of a general combination against the British. How far he was actuated by unwillingness to see the Nána grow too powerful, how far he had been impressed by the conduct of Hartley and his gallant soldiers, cannot be accurately determined[1]. In any case he connived at the escape of Raghuba, who repaired to British protection at Broach with messages of goodwill from his liberator by way of credentials.

In the meantime the Bengal column was delayed by the hostility of various Chiefs in Bundelkhand and by the operations which Colonel Leslie felt himself bound to undertake against them. But Leslie died in October; and his place was taken by Colonel Goddard whom Hastings—now supreme in his own Council—had already chosen as his successor. Urged by pressing appeals from Bombay, Goddard hastened on. He crossed the Narbadá 2nd December, and reached Surat on 6th February, escaping by this promptitude

[1] *v. inf.* p. 197.

from encountering a body of 20,000 cavalry which had been sent from Poona to intercept him. On the 15th April he opened negotiations with the darbár, on the basis of the Treaty of Purandhar, with an additional clause directed against the interference of France. With regard to Sindhia, Goddard was authorised to offer separate arrangements, as the Governor-General was sensible of his humanity in sparing Egerton's force at Wadgáon, and thought he might become a useful ally for the future. But Sindhia had not then quite made up his mind, although he had not scrupled to avow his warm appreciation of the British soldiers.

About this time Sukh Rám Bápu fell into the hands of his enemies, as was suspected by Sindhia's connivance. He was conveyed from one fortress to another, and ultimately died at Ráigarh. Goddard, for his part, avoided any further interference in the domestic affairs of the Maráthás; and, though he was treated personally with the utmost liberality, Raghuba was not again forced upon an unwilling community. The Nána refused to make peace as long as Raghuba was not surrendered; accordingly the British General, who had now been appointed Commander-in-Chief of the Bombay army, prepared for extremities. On the 15th February, 1780, Ahmadábád, the capital of Gujarát, was stormed by the gallant Hartley—now a Lieutenant-Colonel—and on the 29th, Sindhia, accompanied by Holkar, advanced to Baroda as if to attack the British forces.

Still no overt act of hostility took place: and the hostages whom Sindhia had retained as security for the fulfilment of the convention of Wadgáon were restored to liberty and came into Goddard's camp on 9th March. Sindhia even attempted to learn from the General what terms he might expect; but the reply was to ask him to state his own demands. Thus challenged, Sindhia demanded that he should be made Regent at Poona, on behalf of Raghuba's younger son, Bájí Ráo—the same who was afterwards the last of the Peshwás. As nothing serious seemed to be intended, and Sindhia was at the same time making secret overtures to Goddard's native allies, it was determined to read him a fresh lesson, and after repeated attacks he was driven over the Narbadá.

The war, in fact, was becoming a duel between Sindhia and Warren Hastings; and for some twelve months the two ablest men in India faced one another in earnest conflict. The last decisive blow but one was struck in Gwalior, a region which the Sindhias had added to their possessions in North Málwá. The following description of the Gwalior Fort is abstracted from the *Imperial Gazetteer of India*:—

'The fort of Gwalior stands, then, on an isolated rock of sandstone, capped in places with basalt, and having a perpendicular face. Where the rock is less precipitous by nature it has been artificially scarped; so that, in some portions, the upper portion actually projects over the part below. Its greatest length is a mile and a half; its greatest breadth 300 yards;

the maximum height is 342 feet. It contains an old Mughal palace, and was formerly used as a place of confinement, like the Tower of London, for members of the royal family and other prisoners of high rank or important character. In the dismemberment of the Empire it was seized by the Ját Rána of Gohad, now represented by the Máhárána of Dholpur; but Sindhia had lately taken possession of it and strengthened the defences' (*Imp. Gaz.* v. 234 ff.).

Hither on 3rd August 1780 came, invited by the Rána of Gohad, a brisk officer named Popham, instructed by Hastings to stir up a confederation of Játs and Rájputs in Sindhia's rear. Preparing his scaling-ladders in the deepest secrecy, and placing confidence in no one but his able and resolute engineer, Captain Bruce[1], Popham crossed the Chambal at Dholpur, and marched swiftly on Gwalior, whither he sent forward a storming-party of twenty picked men under Bruce, whom he supported in person with a strong reserve. Shod with cotton, to muffle the sound of their footfall, the men reached the foot of the rock, in a dark night, without attracting observation; and, guided by some thieves who knew the place, they lay quiet while the rounds were passing on the walls above. When the lights and voices had passed on they laid their ladders against the rock; and, softly mounting, surprised the guard, whom they overpowered and bound. Popham followed,

[1] Brother to James Bruce, the Abyssinian traveller.

and captured the apparently impregnable fort without losing a single soldier.

The taking of Gwalior had an immediate effect on political ideas and movements. The Náná's agent in the camp of Sindhia wrote to Poona to say that the cause would not have the support of the Delhi Government. As for that Chief himself, he was always swift to take a hint; and he must have felt that, isolated as he now was, and opposed to an adversary whom he had very good reason to believe his master, the friendship of the British might be found of more benefit to him than their hostility, in the furtherance of his ulterior designs. For, if we may judge from subsequent events, Sindhia was already planning a great scheme, of which these foreigners in Bengal were only so far a part as he might utilise them for his purpose. That purpose was the creation for himself of a position of paramount power on the ruins of the Mughal Empire. To that object the relations that he might establish at Poona and Calcutta were subsidiary; Sindhia would not willingly have on his hands any hostility from such powerful neighbours; but he would, so far as lay in his power, enforce respectful treatment, if not positive support. This appears to be the key to his attitude in both directions. He desired no quarrel with Holkar and the Náná, whose benevolent neutrality was almost as important to him as their active support. With regard to Hastings his needs were almost the same;

yet he resolved, if possible, to strike back a monitory, if not a retaliatory, blow before entering into peaceful negotiations. He therefore marched against the British in the Gwalior country, the more hopefully since Popham was gone and Popham's successor, Major Camac, seemed a little inclined to avoid an encounter. But the sagacious Bruce was still there, with another nocturnal surprise. Sindhia's camp was suddenly beaten up; he lost elephants, horses, baggage; but he gained what was worth more than all, a knowledge of the facts of the case that never greatly failed him afterwards.

This affair, 24th March, 1781, was the end of the struggle between Sindhia and Hastings; and it may be noted as much to the credit of one of the antagonists as of the other. Never again, in the weakest period of Shore and Cornwallis, did Sindhia appear in arms against the British or fail in respect to their expressed claims or wishes. It is a prime characteristic of Warren Hastings that whatever he did was done for good; he never built with bad materials or on foundations of sand. It is equally characteristic of Sindhia that he never, when once he had learned them, forgot the limits of his own strength.

On 13th October of the same year Mr. Hastings concluded, through the agency of Colonel Muir, a negotiation in which he accorded to Sindhia the handsome treatment that one able antagonist ought always to know how to give to another. Hastings restored to Sindhia both Gwalior and Ujjain, together with all his previous possessions south and west of the Jumna river; and the only condition of these lavish grants was that Sindhia should do his best to persuade the ministry at Poona to consent to make peace[1].

The result was the Treaty of Salbái (17th May, 1782); an instrument whose importance may be easily overlooked, but which made an epoch in history. For it was by means of that treaty that, without annexing a square mile of territory, the British power became virtually paramount in the greater part of the Indian peninsula, every province of which, with the one exception of Mysore, acknowledged that power as the great universal peacemaker. It was no mean title.

Although Sindhia signed in May on behalf of the confederation for which he acted, yet the Nána, with his customary caution, delayed the ratification as long as possible. He still cherished the hope that the British might be persuaded to restore Salsette; and even went so far as to give currency to a rumour that the Peshwá's Government was negotiating a separate treaty with Haidar 'Alí of Mysore. To such a threat the British could not but be extremely sensitive, seeing that this ancient enemy was still plotting the ruin of their cause with Bussy and other of their inveterate foes. But the death of Haidar in December tore the last shred of this pretence; and before the end of the month the treaty received the signature of the Nána and the seal of the Confederacy.

[1] *v. inf.* p. 202.

The general pacification, however, was incomplete without the adhesion of Mysore, where Tipú the son of Haidar 'Alí had succeeded to his father's possessions and passions if not to his abilities. Such was the eagerness of the Madras Government for peace that it sent representatives to the camp of Tipú prepared to undergo whatever insults the barbaric malice of that modern Hannibal might choose to offer; and it was not till the 10th March, 178 that, amidst circumstances of deep humiliation, Tipú gave a grudging and sullen adhesion to the pacification, by signing the Treaty of Mangalore.

But both sides were equally weary of the war; and Hastings was beginning to set his house in order with an eye to laying down his office and leaving the country. He recognised the real master of the country powers not in Tipú the arrogant, ill-tempered Chief of Mysore, but in the self-restrained and politic soldier of the Maráthás. He therefore condescended to give Sindhia frank explanations of his reasons for confirming the Treaty of Mangalore and for leaving undisturbed the deplorable proceedings of the Madras Government; and he succeeded in showing his intelligent correspondent that it was for the welfare and interest of both of them that things should be as they were.

Nothing, in fact, could give a higher conception of the position to which Sindhia's talents and courage had raised him than the fact that while a statesman such as Hastings could solicit his good offices in the cause of peace, he should in the same affair be vested with plenipotentiary powers by a politician so crafty as the Nána. At the same time the terms agreed upon do credit to his reputation for good sense and moderation. The Gujarát question was left as in 1775, so that the territories of the Gáekwár were preserved from dismemberment; and Raghuba, the restless, was pensioned off handsomely and allowed to choose his own residence. For himself Sindhia secured what he most wanted, a free hand in Central India and Hindustán. By this masterly arrangement he delivered himself, it may be said, from all fear of interruption in his great design. The opposition of the Nána was held in complete check by the ever possible competition of Raghuba and his sons; while the interference of the British was, so to speak, discounted. James Mill [1] professes to suspect something mysterious in the understanding between Sindhia and Hastings at this juncture; but the matter appears plain enough. Hastings had sufficient experience of factious opposition to know that delicate negotiations, such as these undoubtedly were, demanded secrecy; but the general idea at which he was aiming is as clear as possible. The Empire had fallen: the British had taken such portions of it as were required for their commercial purposes: it was to their interest that the rest of the peninsula should be under the rule most conducive to peace and order; and that rule was, evidently, Sindhia's.

The name of Warren Hastings was to Mill what

[1] *History of British India*, vol. v (ed. Wilson).

the mention of the Church was to Gibbon, a disturbing element which made everything with which it was connected appear through a refracting medium. It can hardly be necessary to notice the 'solemn sneer' with which the Treaty of Salbái is regarded by the able historian of British India, whose work is one of the great monuments of our literature notwithstanding such defects. The arrangement was slow, sure, and almost natural in its fitness: it may be almost said to have been tantamount to a temporary partition of the peninsula between the two statesmen who had become its masters. Its direct effects lasted beyond the life of one of the contracting chiefs, beyond the public life of both; indirectly it was the corner-stone of the British Indian Empire. Setting apart the territories of Tipú and the Nizám, Sindhia was free to deal as he chose with all parts not ruled by the British. Hastings, the only British Indian ruler who never made an annexation, secured the interests of his country in the best way by leaving the rest in the hands of his wisest and ablest contemporary. In the great competitive examination which had been going on for many years, Sindhia had come out first and taken all the prizes.

Nor was Hastings content with a merely academic or Platonic approval: to clench the arrangement he sent a British mission to Delhi, as if to publish the alliance to the world and smooth the way for his ally in a path of thorn and pitfall from which he ostentatiously withheld his own footsteps. On that path

Sindhia was now to enter. Hitherto we have seen little but formative circumstance and the quiet tenacity with which he adapted his conduct and character to his surroundings without losing sight of his ultimate object. Henceforth we shall see him working forward by a brighter light and with an ampler record.

CHAPTER IV

Delhi Politics under the Restored Empire

In order that we should fully appreciate the difficulties which had been obstructing Sindhia's great design, we must first look back to 1773 and observe what had been going on in the court and camp of the Emperor Sháh 'Alam since the main army of the Maráthás retired from Hindustán in the hot season of that year. They had left garrisons in Rohilkhand, and they maintained a secret communication with Háfiz Rahmat Khán, the Protector of the Rohillá State. They had also an understanding of the same kind with other Musalmán Chiefs whom they had corrupted, with Zábita Khán for example, and with the courtier named Hissám-ud-daulá—the same who had been their agent in the matter of the Restoration.

The cause of the Ex-Minister, Mírzá Najaf Khán, however, was supported by his old friend the Nawáb, who was a Shia like himself and hereditary Wazír of the Empire. In Warren Hastings the Mírzá had a still more influential friend; so that, when the Nawáb Wazír had determined to press the Rohillás to a final settlement, it was a matter alike easy and important to reinstate the Mírzá in the post from whence Zábita had dislodged him with the aid of Holkar and the Quarter-Master-General.

Háfiz Rahmat was in no hurry to see the Maráthás expelled from Rohilkhand; but he could not help himself. The Nawáb Wazír and Sir R. Barker drove out all their garrisons after a feeble resistance, beating them again in the Doáb, and finally driving them across the Chambal in the month of October. Rohilkhand was saved, in spite of its ruler. The Nawáb now peremptorily demanded the forty *lákhs* which had been the stipulated price of the service which he had performed; but the Protector had no intention to pay, and replied by transparent evasions. A British brigade therefore proceeded to Anúpshahr to occupy Ahmad Sháh's old cantonment; it was commanded by Sir Robert Barker, who was one of the witnesses to the agreement between the Nawáb and the Rohillás[1]. The Mírzá, who had taken refuge in Barker's camp, was at the same time sent back to Delhi, with strong letters of recommendation from the Nawáb and from the British commander; and he resumed his office as Deputy-Wazír. As he was escorted by the Frenchman Médoc and a disciplined body-guard, the intrusive Zábita found it expedient to retire to the Játs of Bhartpur; and Hissám-ud-daulá, whose back-stairs' influence had procured him the administration of the Home-demesnes, was relieved of his charge and called to a strict account; his place being given to

[1] See Trotter's *Warren Hastings*, in this series.

one 'Abdul Ahid Khán, an effeminate Kashmírian who took the title of Majíd-ud-daulá [1]. Manzúr 'Alí Khán was at the same time appointed Názir—Steward—of the Imperial Household. The fortified palace of Agra was entrusted to a Persian immigrant named Muhammad Beg Khán.

So far, therefore, it might seem that any scheme of creating a Hindu power on the Jumna would be difficult, if not hopeless. The Maráthás had been driven out of Hindustán by a Musalmán combination, almost as decisively as had been done by Ahmad Sháh twelve years before. And the present Muhammadan league had the support of the new and mysterious power that was now forcing its way, by battle and intrigue, in all the regions of the lower Ganges. Goddard and Popham were yet to come; but the British had already beaten to submission the powerful Nawáb Wazír, and were now giving him support and active aid. The mere humiliation of the Court of Poona Sindhia could have endured; he would be able to bear any disappointments experienced by the Nána with unruffled resignation. But it might well have daunted him to find a strong and virtuous Persian nobleman in possession of the resources of a restored Empire, with an indefinite prospect of support from the hereditary Wazír, master of the rich and

[1] *Majíd* = 'illustrious.' Titles terminating in *daula* (more properly *daulat*) indicate the second grade in Neo-Mughal Peerage: those in *mulk* being the first. *Arkán-i-daulat* = 'Pillars of the State,' meant nobles in general, or 'Peers of the Realm.'

populous province of Oudh, and strengthened by British bayonets.

The Mírzá's next step was to obtain the sanction of the Emperor to the foreclosure of Rohilkhand. Vehement denunciations of Warren Hastings for his share in this transaction have been so long and so generally accepted that the real nature of it has been almost overlooked. The province of Katahr was as much a part of the Empire as the *Súbah* of Agra; and it had been held, within living memory, by the nobleman who, afterwards transferred to the Deccan, availed himself of the weakness of the Empire to found a hereditary power there. But not one of these so-formed powers, neither this of the Nizám in the Deccan, nor those of the Nawábs of Bengal and Oudh, had any legal base but in patents from the Imperial Chancery, which were as much liable to revocation as any other administrative order. When, therefore, the Patháns, about the year 1743, took advantage of the havoc produced at Delhi by Nádir Sháh to seize the province, they no more made it their own than the Játs did with the fortified palace of Agra and surrounding districts. The latter Najíb-ud-daulá had been able to dispossess; and the Mírzá kept them away by defending the country with his own unaided forces; but the Patháns remained in Katahr; they changed its name to Rohilkhand; they exercised sovereign powers in it, though in a most anarchic fashion, and they had, as we have seen, illusively promised to join in a league against the Maráthás and to pay for the expulsion of the latter in cash.

It now appeared that these Rohillá Patháns were both unable and disloyal. They could not govern the province that they had usurped, nor could they resist the Maráthás; and they would not pay those who came to their assistance. It was therefore a fair political question whether this inefficient military colony should be allowed to continue in possession of a province on which they brought nothing but ruin, or whether it should be transferred to a strong neighbour who was also the highest officer in the Empire. With the action of Mr. Hastings we have here no concern; but the candid reader has now the means of referring to the records of the Calcutta Foreign Office, where he will find materials for drawing his own conclusion[1]. That Shujá-ud-daulá was actuated by personal ambition is only to say that he was an ordinary politician with plenty of human nature about him. He had performed the stipulated service, he had not received the stipulated price, and he was very glad of the opportunity afforded him by the repudiation. That is the worst that can be said of this transaction; and it is very little to its discredit regard being had to the public morality of India at that time. In January, 1774, the Wazír made his last appeal for payment; and on 12th April entered Rohilkhand, supported by a British brigade. The following is the contemporaneous

[1] See Prof. Forrest's *Selections*, published at Calcutta (1890).

native account of the state of the country, as recorded by the historian of the Rohillás:—

'A surprising state of animosity and discord existed in Rohilcund, and each person was earnestly bent on the eradication of his neighbour.' He adds that life and property were unprotected and the lands held at a rack-rent. It was high time that such a condition of affairs should cease. The Protector had no support from the general population. The Emperor, who had by this time given the Wazír a patent of investiture, moved in support at the head of some of his own troops. The British sent a good brigade of their regular troops from Bengal. On the 23rd April the Protector was attacked by the allies, and overthrown after a desperate resistance in which he lost his life. The victory was attributed to the British contingent, of whose artillery a native author says that 'nothing can withstand it save a particular interposition of Providence.' The Protector was himself cut in two by a chain-shot from those 'dreadful' batteries.

The Nawáb Wazír, Shujá-ud-daulá, did not long survive his new acquisition; for he died on 29th January, 1775. He was succeeded in his possessions and honours by his son Ásaf-ud-daulá, a weak and heartless voluptuary, who never left his province or took any avoidable part in public affairs. Mírzá Najaf was left to carry on the duties of an absentee Chief almost unaided. His first operations were against the Bhartpur Játs, whom he encountered at

Barsána, between Mathura and Bhartpur. European officers were serving on both sides; besides Médoc, the Mírzá's infantry was led by the Count de Moidavre, and the Chevaliers de Creçy and du Drenec—the latter a man of whom we shall hear again hereafter. On the Ját side the attack was begun by the brigade of Reinhardt, or Sombre, with volleys of musketry and repeated showers of grape from the field-pieces. The Mírzá was wounded, but he charged the enemy's line with his cuirassiers; and Sombre, after his custom, slowly drew off his men, forming them up under the protection of his guns: next day he joined the victor. Two of the strongest places were besieged and captured before Midsummer; and the complete ruin of the Játs was probably averted only by a diversion caused in the Mírzá's rear by the irrepressible Zábita. That faithless son of Islám was never disposed to leave a stone unturned; and he had now engaged Sikh assistance in another snatch at power. The Mírzá on hearing of this returned to Delhi just in time to save the Emperor from being attacked in his palace; he then proceeded northward to chastise Zábita and his infidel associates. The Emperor himself followed with a brigade contributed to his aid by the Nawáb 'Asaf-ud-daulá; and Zábita had to keep company with the Sikhs and retreat with them over the Jumna to Pánípat. Here an engagement of some severity took place, without any decisive result. Next day Zábita contrived to conciliate the commander of the Oudh brigade, a eunuch named Latáfat Khán, by whose aid he obtained his pardon on condition of retiring to his fief in the Upper Doáb; the 'Fifty-two Parganás' which now form part of the Sahâranpur and Muzaffarnagar districts.

In 1777 the Mírzá retired to Agra, attended by Sombre, who had joined his service after the battle of Barsána and taken over the post of Médoc: the latter, in 1780, retired to Europe: the Governor of the Fort was, like the Mírzá himself, a Persian immigrant, whose name was Muhammad Beg Hamdáni ('of Hamadan'). In Oudh 'Asaf-ud-daulá, sunk in vice and cruelty, was beginning that course of misrule which eventually led to the ruin of his line. Sháh 'Alam, immured in the palace of his ancestors, became daily more indolent and yielding: in 1778 indeed his constant counsellor Majíd-ud-daulá led him to an abortive attack upon Jaipur, where it was hoped to gain some money by requisition; but the quest proved barren. A military governor being sent to the Sutlej was killed by the Sikhs, about the end of the year; and to punish this offence Majíd, who had no experience of war, led an expedition into the Punjab which was beaten, driven back on Delhi, and only saved by the exertions of the European gunners. In the beginning of 1779 the Upper Doáb was accordingly overrun by the victorious Sikhs, who laid the country waste and even cut down the trees. Majíd did nothing beyond opening negotiations with Madhoji Sindhia to whom he held out hopes of obtaining Bengal, Behar and Orissa whenever the British could be expelled. Sindhia was not then on good terms with the British, as we have seen, but he had an inkling of what they could do; and he did not look upon the present offer as having a more practical character than bargaining for the skin of an unslain bear. He knew the strength of the Mírzá, though at a distance, much better than did the Kashmírian on the spot; and the negotiations came to nothing.

But the contemptuous abstention of the Mírzá was not proof against the distress of his sovereign and of the people whom that sovereign was too weak to protect. From the walls of Delhi men could see the smoke of burning villages, when suddenly the Mírzá's approach became known. Majíd was put into close arrest, and his wealth, acquired by peculation, was confiscated to the public treasury. A strong force was sent to check the Sikhs, under command of the minister's nephew, Mírzá Shafi'. Encountering the disciplined troops of the Mughal minister, the Sikhs were defeated, near Mirath (Meerut) with a loss of 5000 men, and the survivors hurriedly retreated to the Punjab.

Profiting by experience the Mírzá resolved to remain at Court, and Sombre having died, the command of his brigade devolved on his concubine[1], who was baptized by the Romish priest there in 1781 by the style of 'Joanna Nobilis.' This is the remarkable woman known in the nineteenth century as Begam

[1] Reinhardt's lawful wife survived him, and so did his issue by her; but she was insane and the son a minor.

Sombre, or Samru, of Sardhana. Sombre's tomb is still to be seen in the Catholic cemetery at Agra.

The Mírzá himself deceased on 26th April, 1782. Resolute in adversity and merciful in success, free from cruelty or falsehood and possessed of that genuine courtesy which proceeds from natural benevolence, he left a fatal vacuum in the politics of Hindustán. The succession to his office and his property was unscrupulously fought out between his nephew, Mírzá Shafi', and a favourite follower, Afrasyáb Khán. The former was shot in a professedly friendly interview in the end of September 1783; and Afrasyáb obtained his desire in becoming the administrator of a ruined country under an incapable sovereign. A heavy famine now fell upon Hindustán, by reason of two years of previous drought: the year (1840 *Sambat*) is still commemorated, in popular tradition, as the *Chálisa* ('The Forty'). On the 13th of May, 1784, wheat was selling at Lahore for about ten times the customary price. A witness who had been in Sindhia's army (afterwards the famous Colonel Jas. Skinner, C.B.) used to relate that so reduced was the number of human beings, so utterly cowed their spirit, that only a few villages were left, scattered at wide intervals and deprived of intercommunication by the tigers who prowled upon the roads. Another contemporary has recorded that wild beasts preyed upon starved bodies in open daylight.

Amid all these horrors there was still a yearning

for national unity and a respect for the eclipsed power of the Imperial line. 'Such,' wrote an intelligent foreign observer, 'was the respect for the House of Taimur that, although the whole peninsula had been gradually withdrawn from its direct authority, there was not a prince in India who dared call himself "King." Sháh 'Alam was still seated on the throne of the Mughal, and all was still done in his name' (*Gen. de Boigne's Memoirs*).

Such was the grand prize for which Indian politicians were contending, of whom one alone had understood the secret. The British might have had it, perhaps; but they thought their time not come. 'The business of assisting the Sháh,' so wrote the envoy of Hastings in December, 1783, 'must go on if we wish to be secure in India, or regarded as a nation of faith and honour.' Hastings was not deaf to these considerations; but, for various reasons, he was unable to put them into action. He therefore encouraged the only competent substitute. Sindhia, as already stated, had been allowed to recover Gwalior and occupy Gohad; and had been encouraged by Warren Hastings to take his own course in the affairs of Hindustán. On the 27th March, 1784, the Governor-General arrived at Lucknow, where he had an interview with the Heir-apparent to the Empire who had come to seek his protection. Hastings considered the prince's case with his habitual patient courtesy, and granted him an annuity. But, in regard to politics, he could only advise the prince to have recourse to 'Madhoji Sindia.' The movements of that astute politician now began to occupy general attention. On the 18th April the *Calcutta Gazette* contained an announcement to the effect that 'We learn that Sindia is going on a hunting party . . . we also learn that he will march towards Bundelkhand.' In point of fact he meant quite otherwise; he was to march towards Agra, and to hunt bigger game than even tigers.

The *Calcutta Gazette* continued to give news from Hindustán. While Sindhia was encamping on the Chambal to wait on events, the *Gazette* for 10th May informed its readers that 'his Majesty has signified by letters to the Governor-General and Mahárájá Sindia that he will march towards Agra.'

Ever since the ratification of his negotiations with Colonel Muir, Sindhia had done little to win the confidence of the Nána. While carefully watching events in Hindustán, for his own interest, he had never omitted an opportunity of playing on the anxieties of his less adventurous colleague at Poona. He had affected to give consideration, if not actual credit, to the claims of an impostor who pretended to be the famous Bháo escaped from the slaughter of Pánípat; of that pretender, however, the Regency made short work. Then Sindhia professed great anxiety for the interests of a more dangerous claimant, the restless Raghuba; and when that troubler of the Deccan was allowed to settle as a pensioner at Kopárgáon, in Khándés, Sindhia professed to be extremely solicitous for Raghuba's welfare; and he was generally suspected of fomenting intrigues for securing the succession to the Peshwáship for one of Raghuba's sons.

In all this there was an element of real policy blending with a certain amount of good-humoured malice. But with the ratification of the Treaty of Salbái came an opening for wider views and higher aims. The faithless Kashmírian Majíd-ud-daulá had, as we have seen, already attempted to obtain Sindhia's co-operation in some crude scheme that he was forming for putting himself into the place of Mírzá Najaf as Prime Minister and Commander-in-Chief at Delhi, in return for which he had proposed to join Sindhia in an attack upon the British in Bengal. There is no evidence that Sindhia had any wish to join in such undertakings; nor is it at all likely that he would have accepted the Kashmírian's offer or consented to play Mephistopheles to such a feeble Faust. Nevertheless, the Mírzá found out enough to warrant him in removing Majíd-ud-daulá from office; and, for the rest of his life, his authority was undisturbed. As we have seen, the Mírzá died in April 1782; and the attention of Sindhia at once became seriously fixed on Delhi politics. At the end of 1784 he obtained the services of M. de Boigne, whom he sent into Bundelkhand at the head of two disciplined battalions in company with a miscellaneous force under a native general. But in the intervening period he kept an anxious gaze upon the northern horizon, uncertain as yet how to read the omens.

As if to remove every scrap of difficulty, however, all parties united to invite his interposition, and the treacherous but incapable Afrasyáb especially sought his assistance. Muhammad Beg, the actual murderer of Mírzá Shafi', had committed the felonious deed under Afrasyáb's instructions; and was in consequence making himself exceedingly unpleasant, taking possession of Agra on his own account. Then to complete the perilous circle that was closing around him, the minister next attacked Majíd-ud-daulá, the Emperor's Kashmírian favourite, who was by this time quite incapable of any mischief, however petty, and was moreover connected with the Emperor by ancient personal ties. With gratuitous violence, Afrasyáb now arrested the valetudinarian old courtier and subjected him to confiscation and close imprisonment. The Emperor, irritated and alarmed, shut himself up and refused to accompany the arrogant minister on his approaching journey to Agra, where Muhammad Beg refused to give up possession of the fort.

Afrasyáb marched therefore without the sanction of his sovereign puppet; and, on arrival at Agra, encamped under the walls and awaited the coming of Sindhia. In October, 1784, Sindhia arrived, had a friendly interview with the minister, pitched his camp as near as possible, and began to concert matters for an assault upon the rebel garrison.

Three days later Afrasyáb was stabbed in his tent by Zain-ul-abidin, brother to the late Mírzá Shafi'. As the murderer escaped punishment, though known to be a refugee in the Maráthá camp, it was at once conjectured that the murder, though certainly not unprovoked, might not have been committed without suggestion from Sindhia. The truth cannot be positively known; the suspicion may possibly—nay, probably—have been little more than the outcome of the ordinary question *Cui bono?*

In the absence of positive evidence there is nothing but conjecture to aid us in considering whether or no a certain historic character was guilty of any particular crime. The manner of Afrasyáb's death would have been a reproach to Sindhia if it were brought home to him. But it would have been, so far as the record shows, an isolated instance in a life otherwise free from cold-blooded atrocity. From Grant Duff's remarks it may fairly be inferred that not only is there no convincing reason for charging Sindhia with the instigation of this murder, but that the best informed of his contemporaries never suspected him; and the actual assassin had a sufficient motive, in revenge for the murder of his brother. It is true that Sindhia does not appear to have made any attempt to punish him; but the spirit of those anarchic times would warrant his getting the benefit of the *lex talionis.* We are not entitled to demand of a politician that he shall be independent of the spirit of his time, or be guided by principles of which he had never heard. As for the maxim *Cui bono?* it is doubtless a help to the historical detective; but it is no more an infallible guide for him than for the police of daily life.

That Sindhia benefited by Afrasyáb's death is, no doubt, true. All the Chiefs present in camp at once waited on him, and by common consent acknowledged his supremacy. He held an informal darbár and accepted their assurances of support. He then broke up from Agra, leaving Muhammad Beg in temporary possession of the fort. Proceeding to Delhi, he presented himself to the Emperor and offered his services, obtaining in return two patents. The one contained the appointment of the Peshwá to be Vicegerent of the Empire; the other vested in himself the command of the army as Deputy to the Peshwá. As a guarantee for the pay of the troops the provinces of Delhi and Agra were assigned to him, but they were made subject to a primary charge of sixty-five thousand *rupees* as a monthly payment for the household and personal expenses of the Emperor. Thus far the great game had been won.

NOTE.—As the relations between Hastings and Sindhia just before, and just after, the Treaty of Salbái had a great influence upon the later and greater events of Sindhia's career, it may be well to refer the reader to Wilson's sensible note on the subject (vol. v, p. 15). It is plain that the character of Sindhia had inspired Hastings with respect. His own generous heart had impelled him strongly to take active measures for the relief of the unfortunate Emperor, who was the legitimate source of all power in India, and especially of that of the British in Bengal. Hastings afterwards admitted that there was a time when he 'would have afforded effectual assistance to Sháh 'Alam, if power had been granted,' though he was then deterred by the opposition of his Council: and the admission is fully corroborated by his despatches of the time. But he came afterwards to see, in the deplorable weakness of the Emperor, reasons for being unwilling to expose his employers to an uncertain pecuniary burden for such an object, and to deem it more prudent and more to the advantage of the Emperor himself, that his protection should be left to Sindhia. 'I declare,' he said, in defending himself against the charges framed by the House of Commons, 'that I entered into no negotiations with Madajee Sindia (*sic*) for delivering the Mogul into the hands of the Maráthás: but I must have been indeed a madman if I had involved the Company in a war with the Maráthás because the Mogul, as his last resource, had thrown himself under the protection of Sindia.' That Hastings, as a matter of fact, thought Sindhia likely to be a humane and efficient protector is shown in Wilson's note referred to; and the result supported his belief. So long as Sháh 'Alam was content with Sindhia's protection he enjoyed security and comfort.

CHAPTER V

SINDHIA'S FIRST ADMINISTRATION

UNQUESTIONABLY, these events made a complete revolution in the position of Mádhava Sindhia, changing still more the position of all institutions and men in any way connected with him. Up to the time of which we are now treating he had always transacted public affairs in the name of the Court of Poona, even when in reality acting on his own behalf; so that, as we are informed by Sir John Malcolm, his very javelin-men (*chaubdárs*) were enrolled as servants of the Peshwá (*Central India*, i. 123). Now, concentrated in Hindustán, Sindhia's power became, virtually and almost nominally, that of the Mughal Empire; and, whenever patents were issued, they came as orders of the Sháh, the titles of the Peshwá and Sindhia being added as those of mere ministerial officers. No man was ever less exacting of forms and ceremonies when he himself only was concerned, for he loved reality, and trusted his own power to guard and enforce it; but, when it came to imposing upon weaker minds, Mádhava was almost histrionic in his use of rite and pageant. If the British saw fit to regard him as an independent prince he could not hinder them; indeed, such was their crude and ill-bred way of diplomatic action, which he might deplore but could not rectify. But, rightly viewed, he was but a poor Patel and lucky menial, whom a too-bountiful Providence had endowed with the means of serving his master in a higher sphere: his master and he being, in their widely-differing degrees, both ministers of an august monarch. The Lord of the Known World and Asylum of the Universe was for the moment inconvenienced by the disloyal conduct of some of his subjects; let his faithful servants unite their humble efforts for his Majesty's relief, and all would yet be well.

In all this our hero might sometimes overdo his part. But it does not follow that an actor fails to understand realities because he wears rouge and drapery upon the stage: Sindhia thought that truth in her nakedness could not be usefully or decorously shown; but he seldom ignored fact in his own personal action; and it was a good deal by virtue of that combination that he managed his contemporaries without participating their delusions, and enjoyed the prerogatives of despotism with a minimum of its disadvantages. The humility assumed by Sindhia, however, was far from disarming the jealousy of Holkar and the Nána; and Grant Duff assures us that at no time in his life was the successful adventurer so much off his guard. Indeed, it is evident from an incident presently to occur that

Sindhia was for a moment over-elated by his sudden elevation.

As we have already observed, there was one set of his Majesty of Delhi's subjects whose brutal frankness would not be deceived, and who not only called a spade a spade, but were not above using spades with their own hands. These were the British, led by Hastings. But that undeceivable politician left India in February 1785, and his successor, Sir John Macpherson, was a man of business and, apparently, nothing more. Here seemed to Sindhia a favourable opportunity for trying a fresh experiment; it was possible that the tenacious hold on the provinces, which the Sháh had abandoned in 1771, was a personal characteristic of the departed Governor, and that his successor might have more respect for forms and phrases. Mádhava accordingly caused it to be understood that his Majesty had it in contemplation to demand payment of the tribute guaranteed by the treaty under which the East India Company obtained the 'Diwání' of the eastern districts. This tribute had been for some time unliquidated, but it might soon become necessary to call for the arrears and a pledge of future punctuality.

While thus preparing the provision of the future, Sindhia was not idle in making the best use of means already at his disposal. Mention has already been made of a European officer whom he had sent with two battalions into Bundelkhand for the suppression of some troubles in that region. As M. de Boigne is destined to appear henceforth as Sindhia's ablest and most efficient servant, it will be proper to explain more fully the origin of their connection: which can fortunately be done, at almost first-hand, from information supplied to Captain Grant Duff by the General himself.

In 1783 Sindhia, in virtue of the Treaty of Salbái, was engaged in recovering possession of some of the Gwalior country; and in the course of these operations was besieging the fort of Gohad belonging to a Ját prince, now represented by the Máhárána of Dholpur. While thus employed he learned that his enemy was concerting a plan for the raising of the siege in which he had been offered assistance by a European traveller, who was the friend and correspondent of Mr. Sangster, the superintendent of the Ráná's gun-foundry. Sindhia perceived the merit of the plan, and traced it to de Boigne, the traveller in question. He found that this gentleman was the bearer of letters of introduction from Warren Hastings, in virtue of which he was endeavouring to obtain service with the Jaipur State. He complained to Hastings, who at the same time received a letter from de Boigne, in which the latter asked permission from the Governor-General to accept an offer of service which had been made him by the Rájá of Jaipur. Anxious to avoid complications with Sindhia, the Governor-General wrote to de Boigne inviting him to return to Calcutta and explain his projects in a personal interview. With this invitation de Boigne judged it proper to comply; and, on his return to the Upper Provinces, he took service not with Jaipur but with Sindhia himself. He came as far as Lucknow in the suite of the Governor-General, who in all likelihood approved of the plan.

The gain to Sindhia was enormous: it is hardly an exaggeration to say that Benoît de Boigne was worth at least 50,000 men to his service. Originally an officer in the regiment of Lord Clare in the King of France's Irish Brigade, he had studied the art of war in that army, and afterwards in the army of Catherine of Russia engaged with the Turks in the Levant. Being taken prisoner, he was sold as a slave at Constantinople, but ultimately escaped and got to India overland, with letters of introduction to Lord Macartney—then Governor of Madras. He obtained a commission in the 6th Madras Native Infantry, a corps which was destroyed in Baillie's disaster, but de Boigne was fortunate enough to be on detachment and so escaped the loss of life or liberty which befel his brother officers. Soon after he resigned the service and came to Calcutta, recommended by Macartney to Hastings. So far he had come to the confines of middle age without finding a permanent career for his courage and ability. But the rolling-stone appeared now to be in a fair way to settle and gather moss. His original scheme in coming up the country had been to make his way through Persia, and to approach his old mistress the Czarina with all the information he could collect relative to India and

Central Asia: a great design which might have been attended by important consequences. But the favour of Hastings, and the reception that he now obtained from Sindhia, induced him once more to change his plans. Impressed by the recommendations of the Governor-General, who had noticed with pleased approval the docility with which the adventurer had obeyed his wishes, Sindhia had been further disposed towards de Boigne by the soldierly knowledge and originality displayed in the plans of the latter for the relief of Gohad.

De Boigne was therefore engaged, and was allowed to bring into the service another *quondam* antagonist, the Scotsman Sangster also: and while the one was put in charge of the gun-foundry, the other was commissioned to raise a small infantry force in imitation of the little legions of Sombre and Médoc.

About this time, too, Sindhia had the further satisfaction of being relieved from the hostility of Muhammad Beg, the dislodging of whom had been the ostensible object of his late meeting with Afrasyáb at Agra. When that meeting ended so tragically, the Beg's followers began to see that power was devolving upon abler hands; the garrison melted away, till the Beg was fain to surrender a fortress he could no longer man and enter the service of Sindhia: this took place 27th March, 1785. All that now remained of the once great possessions of Mírzá Najaf was the town of Koil with the adjoining fort of Alígarh, where the family of Afrasyáb held out in hope of good terms. They were not doomed to disappointment. A force was sent to which Alígarh surrendered, an estate being settled by Sindhia for the maintenance of Afrasyáb's son and the family.

In the midst of these easy triumphs appeared proof that, even in its more quiet moods, the British Government would brook no pressure upon the question of money. The following plain sentences appeared in the *Calcutta Gazette* of 12th May, 1785:—

'We have authority to inform the public that, on the 7th of this month[1] the Governor-General received, from the Emperor Shah Aulum and Maha Rajah Madagee Sindia, an official and solemn disavowal of demands . . . for the former tribute of Bengal . . . Mr. Anderson[2] was instructed to inform Sindia that his interference in such demands would be considered in the light of direct hostility . . . and . . a disavowal of claims advanced unjustly and disrespectfully insisted upon.'

These few sentences are enough to show how firmly our precursors in India could act, even at a time when they were weak in men and munitions of war and were restrained from aggressive measures by

[1] It is not clear how this disavowal was expressed; the *Gazette*, in an omitted passage, says that the Sháh and Sindhia made it 'under their respective seals,' as if Sindhia were at that time regarded as a separate power.

[2] Mr. Anderson was the British 'Resident' at Sindhia's headquarters—then, perhaps, at Mathura. The Envoy accredited to the Court of Delhi was Major Brown. It was Anderson who had negotiated the treaty of Salbái, and he would be *persona grata* at Sindhia's *darbár*.

the most peremptory and positive order from the Home Government. It appears, from the same *Gazette*, that Mr. Anderson had already anticipated the orders of his Government; and had founded his first remonstrances on something said, with Sindhia's approval if not by Sindhia himself, at a darbár of the Delhi Court where the Envoy, Major Brown, was taking leave of the Sháh. It is most creditable to the good temper and judgment of Sindhia that immediate explanations were offered; and they were such, in the language of the official organ, 'as must eventually strengthen the alliance with the Mahrattas . . . and secure the general tranquillity of India.'

The Patel, such has always been Sindhia's usual designation among the natives, was now supreme in Hindustán. The disunited Mughal Chiefs were for the moment submissive; and a garrison under Sindhia's orders kept guard over the Emperor in the 'Red Castle' of Sháh Jahán. His Majesty the Sháh, however, took the field in the military operations about Agra; at the termination of which he returned to Delhi, while his powerful minister retired to Mathura, a holy place of the Hindus and henceforth one of Sindhia's most favoured residences.

Among the many circumstances which, at this period, conduced to the prosperity of the Patel and to the tranquillity of his newly acquired territories in Hindustán was the quiescence of Takújí Holkar. Throughout all the events that had followed the death of Malhár Ráo, 1764, the forces of Takúji, both physical and moral, had been so inferior to those of his old comrade Sindhia as to compel him to adopt a secondary rank alike in the politics of Málwá and of Hindustán. There was no hostility between them; but Holkar's subordinate position and second-rate mind combined to produce this effect: a brave and trustworthy agent, he seemed at this time one of those men who, often to their own real credit, are readily persuaded to abstain from undertakings for their own exclusive aggrandisement. At the time we have now to deal with Holkar was engaged, as a servant of Ahalya Bai and an officer under the Peshwá, in carrying out the policy of the Poona darbár in operations against Tipú Sultán, son of the deceased Haidar Alí; and after the conclusion of those operations he resumed, in his usual dutiful way, his attendance upon the widow of his late master's son. There, however, his stay was short; for he was called on to aid in the settlement of Bundelkhand. This province had long been in a very disturbed state; and the Peshwá now determined to bestow it on a regular feudatory as had been done with so much success in Málwá and Gujarát. The Chief selected was a bastard Musalmán, named Alí Bahádur, son of the late Peshwá, Bájí Ráo, by a Muhammadan concubine. Formerly an officer in Sindhia's army, he had deserted; but, with customary good temper and sense, Sindhia made no opposition to his establishment in Bundelkhand. Here he became the founder of that House, of 'Nawábs of Bánda,' who, opposing the British, were mediatised by Lord Hastings; and whose last representative was deposed for misconduct in 1857.

For these and other services Holkar was granted a share in the profits of that most commercial of Empires founded by the Maráthá confederacy: and out of these claims seeds ripened which were to germinate hereafter into misunderstanding, war, and ultimate disaster. Yet it is remarkable that of all the Chiefs of those days there were none whose power has come to be more established than the founders of the States of Gwalior and Indore.

One of the very first cares of Sindhia was to provide a safe road from his southern estates in Málwá, *viâ* Gwalior, to Delhi: and one of the strongholds on the way was the fort of Raghugarh belonging, as it still does, to the head of the Kechi Clan of Chauhán Rájputs. So far back as 1780, Sindhia had begun hostilities against the then Chief, Rájá Balwant Singh; and he now sent a column to besiege this fort, under Muhammad Beg, whom he was anxious to provide with employment.

A short account of the Kechi tribe of Raghugarh will be useful as illustrating the mutual relations and different proceedings of a very noble clan of Hindus and the Maráthás, who, though Hindus who attained to great distinction, were certainly not distinguished by character or conduct such as we are accustomed to connect with the idea of nobility. The

Kechis were a clan of Chauhans, as were the Sisodias of Méwar, or Udaipur; and the two clans emulated each other in leadership and in examples of punctilious purity. Of both divisions, that of Udaipur and that of Raghugarh, it was the common boast that they had never followed the lead of Amber (Jaipur) and Marwar (Jodhpur) in allowing the Mughal Sultáns to take brides from among their daughters, and had chosen to endure the severest persecution from the Imperial Government rather than submit to such degradation. Of the two Udaipur was usually the most conspicuous and powerful; nevertheless, Jai Singh, son and successor of Rájá Balwant, in a letter which he wrote, a few years later, to propose to the British authorities an alliance against Sindhia, asserted that he was the true Chief of all Rájputs and hereditary 'Hindupat,' or sovereign of the Hindus. This claim was probably based on the doctrine of Rájput heralds, that the Kechis of Raghugarh were lineally descended from the famous Pirthi Ráj, or 'Rai Pithaura,' whose exploits are the subject of Chand's celebrated epic, and whose fortifications are still visible near the Kutb Minár at Old Delhi. About the middle of the eighteenth century, while the Maráthás were occupying the neighbouring districts, the then representative of this proud House was the centre of a general attack by no less than thirteen confederate Chiefs. Over this league, however, he prevailed; and this gave the Peshwá, Bálají Bájí Ráo, so high an idea of his power that his alliance was sought for the Maráthá cause. Having little reason to love his Rájput neighbours, he accepted the offer, became a constant companion of the Chiefs of the Holkar and Sindhia clans who settled in Málwá, and left his son Balwant apparently strong and prosperous at his death—about 1780.

It was this Chief against whom Sindhia now resolved to employ Muhammad Beg and his levies: on his first accession, indeed, Sindhia had got him into his power; but a subordinate Kechi Chieftain, Sher Singh, had, by a singular expedient, obtained the Rájá's release. Without proclaiming war, or sending a single soldier into Sindhia's territories, some of which lay close by, Sher Singh deprived Sindhia of all profit from his new annexation. For he at once sent orders to all the husbandmen of the Raghugarh State—or Kechiwára—to leave their fields untilled and betake themselves to the neighbouring State of Bhopál, where he had made arrangements with the ruling Minister to protect and provide for them. The Minister was a Musalmán, Chata Khán by name; and it is almost equally singular that he should have sided with the Kechis against an authority professing to emanate from the Mughal Chancery, and that Sindhia should have passed over his conduct without any attempt at punishment. Sindhia's good-tempered forbearance was not at first rewarded. Sher Singh, though abstaining from open attack, was relentless in his ill-treatment of Maráthá Bráhmans who fell into his hands, declaring that it was by their advice that

Sindhia was actuated, but he would teach him how to handle a Rájput principality. And then occurred a pleasing incident, showing the Chauhan chivalry in a favourable light, and giving a gratifying instance of Madhoji's placable though rigorous nature. It happened that the wife of Sindhia, accompanied by the families of some of his officers, was coming from Poona to Mathura; and considerable alarm was felt as to what might happen should Sher Singh, as was quite possible, surprise and cut up the escort. Sindhia, therefore, wrote to Chata Khán, the Bhopal *Diwán*; and at his intercession Sher Singh gave the travellers an unmolested and honourable passage through the country of Kechiwára: and Sindhia acknowledged the courtesy in a handsome letter. Shortly after occurred the peace with Jaipur and Jodhpur, and at the intercession of the Rájás Balwant Singh was, finally, released; but Ambaji Inglia, who was then commanding for Sindhia in Málwá, picked a quarrel with him about ransom, and refused to restore the fort of Raghugarh. Having neither money nor energy Balwant retired to Jaipur, where he ultimately died, and was succeeded by his son Jai Singh, a young man of ruthless but vigorous character.

The rest of the story of Kechiwára does not belong to the life of Mádhava Sindhia. He does not seem to have ventured on contravening the arrangement made in his behalf by Ambáji, nor is the present writer in a position to say with certainty that Ambáji was without justification for his course of action. But it was resented by Jai Singh, a man of more spirit than his father, though he sometimes showed it in a manner so cruel as to be suspected of insanity. He was cordially assisted in his hostilities against Sindhia by Durjan Lál, who had been Rájá Balwant's *Vakil*, or agent, at Sindhia's Court; and these hostilities were maintained long after Mádhava's death.

It was about the same time as the date of Muhammad Beg's expedition to Raghugarh that Mádhava attempted to consolidate his influence at the Mughal Court by inviting the return of Mírzá Jawan Bakht, the Heir-apparent, from Lucknow. We saw that this sensible and virtuous Prince had been left at Delhi by Ahmad, the Duráni Sháh, as ostensible head of the provisional government established there in 1759. Since then he had seen many vicissitudes; and had escaped from the palace during Afrasyáb's tenure of office, and went to Lucknow, about the end of April, 1784. There he had met Mr. Hastings, whose sympathies were warmly excited by the sorrows of the excellent prince, and by whom an annuity of four *lákhs* was granted to him, with a strong recommendation to throw himself on the protection of Mádhava Sindhia, as already mentioned.

But by 1786 Hastings was gone, and Lord Cornwallis had taken charge of Bengal, with power to impose his decisions on an opposing Council, and instructions to purchase peace at any price. There was, apparently, a conflict among some of the agents of the Government as to the means to be employed to this end; but the result was that the Prince was led to conceive suspicions of Sindhia's motives (for which suspicions no grounds ever appeared) and to decline his invitation. The voices calling the British to Delhi were also unheard or unheeded[1]. It may be that the late successes of Haidar and his son, and the tremendous scale of Indian war, both in point of distances to be traversed and hostile forces to be encountered, may have appalled a man accustomed to scientific warfare, like Cornwallis, and not very fortunate at that. The Resident at Lucknow, Major Palmer, had taken a somewhat larger view: Sháh 'Alam was growing old and lethargic, the interests of the Company seemed bound up in those of the Heir-apparent. Whilst he remained under British influence the usurpation of Sindhia was incomplete, and so long as that was so a great danger was avoided.' So wrote Palmer in 1785. In the following year Cornwallis assumed charge; and after attempting the perennially-recurring reformation of Oudh, he found his attention almost exclusively diverted to the Deccan. He evidently considered that, so far as Hindustán was concerned, it was best that Camerina should not be shaken. 'Many,' said the official organ, 'have urged the necessity of upholding the Mogol influence to counterbalance the power of the Hindus; but this should seem bad policy; as we should causelessly become obnoxious and involve ourselves in the interest of a declining State' (*Calcutta Gazette*, 8 March, 1787).

[1] See Mr. Seton Karr's *Cornwallis*, in this series, pp. 16, 17.

The Prince remaining at Lucknow, and the British being permanently bent on withholding payment of tribute and on retaining, for themselves or for the Nawáb, the possession of the ceded provinces, the Patel was left to his own resources for raising the revenues of his newly-acquired territories. He thus was led to the measure of inquiring into the titles under which vast alienations of revenue had been made by persons who, in the recent anarchy, had set up as hereditary holders of fiefs. The subject of free landholding in India is too large to be here analysed in all its details; it must suffice to explain the essential difference between the systems of Asia and Europe. In the latter a partition of the lands among military leaders had, as we know, become general in the tenth century of the Christian era, by virtue of which allodial tenure disappeared, and large estates were formed which, subject to certain regulated burdens and duties, descended from the father to the eldest son and laid the foundation of landed property as it still exists in this country. In India, on the contrary, and in many other eastern countries, the land was claimed by the township, or *commune*, on condition of paying the surplus produce to the public fisc. The payments were collected in a variety of ways; and each being small in itself, the State found its convenience in grouping a number of townships and giving charge of each group either to a farmer who bought the farm at auction, or to a grantee who was to yield a proportion of the produce, in kind, in cash, or in military service. So far as the two systems may seem to have had a not dissimilar origin, except that in India the townships were often too tenacious of existence and of traditional rights to allow the farmer or grantee to reduce their coparcenors to the position of mere tenants-at-will or even copyholders. But the great difference was, after all, not so much in that direction. Had the farms and grants become hereditary it is probable that the proprietary rights and the communities themselves would have ultimately disappeared—as, indeed, they did in Bengal when the Zamíndárs became proprietors. Fortunately a farm, as such, has no tendency to become hereditary, its very essence being the periodical use of a method of auction. As for the grants, they might often be usurped by the heir when the grantee died; or when the Government was not especially weak, a fine might be accepted in lieu of the trouble of dispossessing the usurper. But, happily for the people, such ideas were opposed to state-theories as much as to popular notions. The spirit of Muhammadan polity does not favour the devolution of property by inheritance so as to create a patrician order. In the palmy days, therefore, of the Mughal Empire, a grandee's fiefs were regarded in the light of pay or pension, and were almost invariably resumed at his death.

Such was the origin of the famous 'Jaghire-system,' of which we hear so much in Indian history[1]. And

[1] *Jai-gir*, = 'place-holding,' is the true Persian term. Clive had

it was into the titles of such holdings that Sindhia now ordered inquiry; with the prospect that the incomes were to be resumed in order to be applied to the purposes of the Government where the title was bad and the grantee too weak to contend against the State. The measure was perfectly legal: it wanted no political justification: its timeliness and prudence form a separate question: Sindhia's head was perhaps a little turned by success. The object that he had in view was to organise a standing army, like that of the Company, in lieu of the levies of the *Jaigirdárs*: and the resumption of the fiefs was, in fact, the substitution of a paid and trained force for the services, often imaginary and always weak, of the usurping Barons. But the Patel had to prepare for the hostility of the latter, who had every motive for opposing the change. The Barons on their part prepared for resistance, and were doubtless encouraged by Muhammad Beg, himself a prominent member of their order, who had by this time succeeded in taking the fort of Raghugarh, but remained encamped in the district.

The standing army was meanwhile taking shape: besides de Boigne other professional officers were making their mark, among the best of whom were the Maráthá Ambáji Inglia and Rána Khán, the *quondam* water-carrier who had saved the life of his master after the rout at Pánípat. Thus supported, Sindhia called

an office of this kind, under an imperial patent, by virtue of which he was the landlord of his employer, the East India Company, in the 'Twenty-four Parganás.'

Muhammad Beg from the settlement of Kechiwára, and ordered him to disband his levies. Muhammad Beg evaded compliance; Himmat Bahádur, a Jaigirdár in Bundelkhand, refused to render his accounts, and went into rebellion; the Rájput Chiefs, emboldened by the evacuation of Raghugarh, joined the combination; all Central India seemed about to take fire. The payment of revenue began to be generally repudiated; and Sindhia's communications with Málwá and the Deccan were cut. Rájá Partáb Singh, of Jaipur, called upon the Jodhpur Chief, Mahárájá Bijai Singh, for aid which was given with alacrity; and the confederacy was soon joined by the Rána of Udaipur and other minor chiefs. Almost without warning, and with his army not yet organised, Sindhia suddenly found his authority challenged by a brave host of 100,000 horse and foot, with 400 pieces of artillery. Against this he had to oppose the regular army under Ambáji and Rána Khán, the small corps of M. de Boigne, and the Mughal horse and regular battalions of the Imperial service under the suspicious direction of Muhammad Beg. The latter general was seconded by his nephew, Ismáil Beg, who proved to be the last of the great Mughal immigrant leaders; a man of an indomitable spirit in battle, and a gallant leader of heavy cavalry, but deficient in prudence and in principle.

Sindhia brought this explosion upon himself by one of those errors of judgment to which he was more subject in prosperity than in adversity. He sent a chieftain of his own clan, Raiájí Sindhia, to demand tribute at the gates of Jaipur; and, when the Rájá, confiding in the combinations already effected, derisively refused compliance, it proved that Raiájí had no means of enforcing the demand. The Musalmán courtiers at Delhi rejoiced at the rebuff of their heathen master; even the feeble old Emperor manifested hostility; while, at the same time, he raised open complaints of the arbitrary conduct of his protector, and alleged himself to be ill-treated and inadequately supplied with money. In this general adversity, and when all his resources appeared likely to be insufficient to conduct a successful campaign in Rájputána, Sindhia suddenly found himself forced to detach two strong bodies of troops under Ambáji to encounter an incursion of the Sikhs to the northward of the capital.

He then took the field in person with the remainder of his troops, and marched towards Jaipur, attended by Muhammad Beg, Rána Khán—the ex-waterman—and by the corps of Appa Khándi and de Boigne, lately returned from Bundelkhand. The army so formed was the 'Imperial army,' and moved with something of imperial state: it was therefore the more easily harassed by what had once been the tactics employed against Aurangzeb. It was surrounded, its foragers and stragglers were cut off, and its supplies shortened. It was also in a disunited condition, and consequently not to be trusted for combined action.

In this state it was encountered by the allies at

Lálsot, a village about forty miles south of Jaipur, at the end of May, 1787. Muhammad Beg deserted to the enemy, followed by Ismáil Beg, the Mughal horse, and a quantity of good infantry and artillery. Worsted in three burning days of unequal combat, and surrounded by marauding skirmishers who plundered his camp at night, Sindhia determined to retire.

But, if he had been led into mistakes by the elation of prosperity, he showed no craven spirit against adverse fortune. He retired in good order; sending off his heavy baggage under a strong escort to Gwalior, calling in all his detachments, and falling slowly back upon the friendly country of Bhartpur. Arrived at Díg, he conciliated the Ját Chief by the cession of that fortress—an old possession of the family—and sent an express to Poona earnestly imploring the Nána to send him reinforcements for the common cause of Máháráshtra. This done, he deposited his heavy artillery in the almost impregnable fortress of Bhartpur, and strengthened the garrison of Agra under the command of Lakwá Dáda, one of the most faithful of his native generals.

A translation of the letter written on this occasion to Nána Farnavis will be found in Grant Duff (iii. 24), and it shows the skilful way in which a man apparently at his last resources could appeal to a not wholly friendly colleague without loss of dignity. The Nána appears to have had an ungenerous moment, and to have complied with Sindhia's request reluctantly, only consenting after much delay and with mortifying conditions. He was more prompt afterwards.

The Rájputs did not follow up their success; but a new trouble was not slow to make its appearance. The son of the late Zábita Khán, who died in January, 1785, was that Ghulám Kádir whose ill-treatment in 1772 has been already mentioned, and who was now in the full possession of his father's fiefs at the head of the Doáb and of his father's turbulence, with infinitely more than his father's energy. His ambition, stimulated, perhaps, by an ill-regulated intellect and a mad impulse of vindictiveness, had been held in restraint by the physical and moral supremacy of Sindhia. The moment had now arrived which he had long awaited. While Sindhia was engaged in his difficult struggle with the Rájputs it would be easy to join his forces to those of Ismáil Beg, obtain possession of Agra and Delhi, and strike a blow with success for the cause of Islám and hereditary fiefs. With the Emperor's person in their power they might renew the enterprise of Ghází-ud-dín, and rule Hindustán to the benefit of the faith and of themselves. In communication, therefore, with Ismáil Beg, who was besieging Agra, Ghulám Kádir set out from his northern estates and proceeded to occupy the country round the metropolis.

In the meantime the Rájputs, having digested their late triumphs, proceeded to renew their attack on Sindhia. Surprising a detachment of his army under Ambáji they put it to flight with severe loss, and drove Sindhia to take refuge in the fort of Gwalior.

This season of distress, as de Boigne used afterwards to relate, was also the season of Sindhia's true greatness. But the Savoyard adventurer was wise after the event. For the moment he despaired, though Sindhia did not; and he began to think of quitting a service in which he saw no prospect of wealth or distinction, and joining the famous Claude Martin in business engagements at Lucknow. Sindhia, however, prevailed on him to undertake some farther operations for his deliverance, and de Boigne did not refuse. For the moment master and man remained at Gwalior, where they were tolerably safe, to await events and prepare for a further effort.

The rainy season had now set in, and suspended military operations. But, towards the end of the monsoon, while the Beg was still engaged in the siege of Agra, Ghulám Kádir advanced on Delhi, and encamped at Sháhdara on the left bank of the Jumna, facing the palace of the Mughals. In the city was a Maráthá garrison, which was commanded by Sindhia's son-in-law, called 'The Desmukh,' and by a Muhammadan official called Sháh Nizám-ud-din, whom Sindhia had lately put in charge of the home-demesnes. They opened fire on Ghulám Kádir's camp, a hostility that was promptly returned: and presently, finding that Ghulám Kádir had secured the sympathies and connivance of the Názir and other Mughal officers, they threw up the defence and retired to Ballabgarh, a fort then garrisoned by the friendly Játs.

Ghulám Kádir immediately entered Delhi, and was presented to the Emperor by the Názir, Manzur Ali—a nominee, as may be remembered, of the late Mírzá Najaf Khán. This man had been for some time in correspondence with the rebel, perhaps propitiated by gifts, perhaps affected by the mirage of a Musalmán revival. He now allotted to the young Pathán the quarters in the palace usually reserved for the *Amir-ul-Amara*, or Premier noble. This had been the office held by the original Najíb, and constantly claimed by Zábita; and Ghulám Kádir had set his hard heart upon obtaining it for himself. But the Emperor was not yet fallen so low as to reward a rebel. Aided by Begam Sombre, who hastened to Delhi on hearing of the intended revolution, his Majesty dismissed the Pathán, who retired to his camp. He also raised additional guards, and summoned Najaf Kuli Khán, a former retainer of Mírzá Najaf, from his estate at Rewári, about fifty miles distant. This Chief immediately obeyed the summons; and, on arriving at Delhi, encamped by the Begam, in front of the main gate of the palace, on the 17th November, 1787. A cannonade was then opened on the rebels, who replied by firing shots, of which some fell into the interior of the palace.

Presently a compromise was effected, Sindhia being still in difficulties at Gwalior, and his best troops beleaguered by Ismáil Beg in Agra. Ghulám Kádir was formally invested with the insignia of the office that he coveted. He then marched off to attack Sindhia's fort at Alígarh, which he took after a faint resistance, and thence proceeded to join the Beg before the walls of Agra.

At the end of 1787 Sindhia, having received large reinforcements from Poona, crossed the Chambal at Dholpur, and advanced to the relief of Agra. Ghulám Kádir and the Beg on learning this broke up their camp and marched in search of him. An engagement ensued at the village of Chaksána, in which Rána Khán commanded Sindhia's army, and in which the regular battalions were led by de Boigne; and of the battle which ensued we have that general's own description. He says that the Musalmán leaders fought well, Ghulám Kádir breaking the infantry line of the right wing by a charge of cavalry. Ismáil Beg attempting the same tactics on de Boigne's battalions was received with coolness and success. But the Maráthá horse were no match for the Mughal cuirassiers; the Játs were equally inefficient; and it required all the efforts of the European officers to protect the retreat with their infantry and guns. Rána Khán retreated by night upon Bhartpur, and the enemy resumed the siege of Agra thus vainly interrupted. Shortly after the battle, however, Ghulám Kádir returned to his northern possessions, drawn off by an attack of the Sikhs from across the Jumna, who had been set in motion by emissaries from Sindhia's camp.

The winter of 1787-8 is marked by the curious

appeal of Mírzá Jawan Bakht, the Heir-apparent, for aid from the British. Not feeling any hope of support from Lord Cornwallis, the Prince repaired to Delhi, whence he addressed himself directly to King George III. The letter is part of the history of British India; and is only to be noticed here by reason of the view that it expresses as to the conduct of Sindhia, who is mentioned as vainly desired to 'conciliate the attachment of the old nobility, and to extend protection to the distressed peasantry.' Sindhia is classed with Ghulám Kádir as among the enemies of the Imperial House and of its allies, 'the Rájas and Princes of the Empire'; and the letter closes with a passionate appeal to the British King to 'restore the royal authority, to punish the rebellious, to give repose to the people of God, and to render his name illustrious among earthly potentates.'

Foiled in all attempts to succour his unhappy father, and threatened in life and liberty by the attempts of Ghulám Kádir, the Prince retired to the protection of the British at Benares, where he died on the 31st of May. Idle as the speculation may be, it is hard to refrain from a passing thought as to what might have happened if he could have combined with Sindhia and drawn off the Musalmán leaders from their operations against Agra and Delhi.

Unsupported by the Heir-apparent and the British, Sindhia's fortunes seemed ebbing fast. Attempting to move from Bhartpur to Alwar he was checked by the Jaipur Rája, who drove him back towards Arga. On his way thither he was again attacked by Ismáil Beg and driven in flight across the Chambal. The Jodhpur army defeated Ambáji, and hindered him from bringing help to his master. Receiving fresh reinforcements from the Deccan, however, Sindhia renewed his attempt to raise the siege of Agra where Lakwa Dáda still gallantly held out. A battle ensued near the famous ruins of Fatehpur-Sikri, in which de Boigne's battalions once more bore the brunt, and in which Sindhia was at last successful. Ismáil was routed, and had to escape by swimming his horse through the waters of the Jumna near Agra, the siege of which town was immediately raised after a duration of just twelve months. On the other shore Ismáil found Ghulám Kádir, who had returned, after settling with the Sikhs, and with whom he proceeded to Delhi, where they arrived sometime in June.

In the meanwhile M. de Boigne, weary of a war in which he had all the hard work but nothing of the direction, left the service of Sindhia and took up a business career at Lucknow. Feeling the loss of this invaluable assistant, Sindhia proceeded to take a little repose at Mathura, while the Emperor, whose imbecile intrigues and subterranean hostility had been undermining all his operations, was left to fare as he might with his new associates. His bad feeling towards Sindhia is shown in his son's letter to George III[1].

[1] The letter to George III undoubtedly expresses the Sháh's real feeling towards Sindhia, the writer being then an inmate of his ill-starred father's palace.

But he had shown it in a more active way, at first by secret letters to the Rájput Princes, and afterwards also by openly marching towards Ajmere in the spring. It is true that he did not get any further than Gokalgarh, a stronghold of Najaf Kuli, who had been displaying some insolence. But his expedition was undoubtedly planned in impotent antagonism to Sindhia, being undertaken in pursuance of an invitation from the Jodhpur Rája, professedly supported by the Jaipur Chief, with both of whom Sindhia was then at open war. Gokalgarh surrendered; and the Emperor, satisfied with this petty success, returned to Delhi on the 15th April, accompanied by Himmat Bahádur, another open enemy of the Patel.

CHAPTER VI

SINDHIA AND GHULÁM KÁDIR

IN the main events of this chapter Mádhava had less part than would have been expected. It has always been a question with his admirers why he remained aloof from the sovereign whom he professed to serve, at a time when that most imbecile of monarchs was exposed to insult and ill-treatment from persons to whom he, Sindhia, had been so lately and so fiercely opposed. Two reasons will occur to readers of these pages. Sindhia may not have thought his forces equal to the siege of Delhi, or he may have wished that the Emperor should be taught by bitter experience who were his true friends, and on which side his best interests lay. He did not, we may be sure, calculate on the mad extremes to which the violence of Ghulám Kádir would proceed: he doubtless thought that the persons and property of the descendants of Taimur would be safe in the hands of a gallant soldier, like Ismáil Beg, and a wealthy and high-born noble like Ghulám Kádir. In any case he remained supine at Mathura for three months, during which the passive courage of the fallen sovereign and the brutal violence of his oppressors were without a parallel, and remained so till the French excesses of 1792, and the slow destruction of the unhappy Louis XVI. Grant Duff suggests another reason: 'Sindhia,' he says, 'was still in need of further reinforcements from the Deccan, which Holkar and the Nána were unwilling to supply unless on condition of being admitted to a share of Sindhia's power in Hindustán.'

The revolution at Delhi seemed now complete. The cause of the Crescent was accepted by the Emperor and his court, and by the mob of eunuchs and parasites who thronged the beautiful marble halls and the precincts of the palace, smiling at the efforts of the Christian Begam and the Hindu Patel. The nearest Musalmán rival was a slothful Wazír at Lucknow; Ghulám Kádir was the highest official at Delhi, having lawfully become Premier-noble, thereby gaining an office of undefined character which had often conveyed political power to its possessor. The actual military command was held by Ismáil Beg, whose forces were stationed in the old city of Firoz Sháh Tughlak. It was now the middle of the monsoon. On the 18th July the confederates entered the palace, with fifty men-at-arms, and received *Khilats* (dresses of honour): they then retired, with all the outward marks of respect, to concoct arrangements for a general scheme of plunder, in which Ismáil was to levy requisitions from the city while Ghulám Kádir undertook the spoliation of the palace.

Hints of these intentions, and demands for money

preferred in tones of growing insolence, alarmed the helpless Sháh, who sent, when too late, to implore the help of Sindhia. Early in the morning of the 27th July, Ghulám Kádir left the quarters of the Amir-ul-Amara, and presented himself at the *Diwán Khás*, where he peremptorily demanded an audience. The Sháh accordingly came out of his private apartments —though the hour was but 7 a.m.—and found many courtiers and officials assembling round the faded semblance of the peacock-throne. Citing the authority of Ismáil Beg, the new Premier announced that, in obedience to his Majesty's orders, the army was ready to march on Mathura, and to chase the Maráthás from Hindustán. But, before the campaign could be opened, it would be absolutely necessary to provide for the payment of arrears due to men and officers. Their late services had been required by the State; and it was to the State Treasury that the army must look for payment. This harangue was protracted for some time, and at its conclusion met with applause from the speaker's party headed by the Názir. But Lala Sital Dás, the Treasurer, being sent for to report on the state of the finances, stoutly declared that payment was impossible. It was not for him to appraise the services of the Patháns; all he could say was that his chests were empty. They had seen his Majesty but lately melting down his plate to allow of the raising of a small body of men wherewith to augment his body-guard. There was no money to pay the Patháns.

On hearing this statement Ghulám Kádir assumed an air of indignation, the whole scene having been probably prepared—perhaps concerted with the Názir. Drawing from his bosom a letter from the Emperor (calling for help from Sindhia), which had been intercepted by his police, he ordered his followers to disarm the Sháh and remove him into close custody. The Sháh attempting resistance, Ghulám Kádir drew his sword, and would have cut down the Emperor had not the Názir interposed and persuaded the fallen sovereign to retire quietly to his own apartments. For the next three days he was left there, with the members of his family, entirely without food or attendance, while the Pathán enthroned a feeble recluse whom he entitled Bédar Bakht, and set on foot his long-planned scheme of wholesale plunder.

The Beg, however, proved a difficult accomplice: finding that Ghulám Kádir kept possession of the palace without sending any pay to himself or his men, on whose protection he was dependent, Ismáil's not very lively intelligence began to take alarm. Sending for the heads of the urban community he advised them to provide for their own safety, promising to protect them so long as he might remain, and giving strict charge to his officers accordingly.

Meanwhile Ghulám Kádir proceeded to ransack the palace. The new Emperor was sent to plunder his predecessor, and women were employed to search the ladies of the Imperial family and strip them of their jewelled ornaments. Dissatisfied with the proceeds of these, he fell back upon a notion which seems to have grown in his mind till it became a mere monomania—the idea that the palace contained a hidden treasure, the secret of which was known to the Sháh, and to him only. Most of the atrocities that the Pathán now committed are to be ascribed to this fixed idea of a secret hoard obstinately concealed from him by a wilful but helpless old man.

The prospect of being abandoned by Ismáil Beg, however, and of losing the protection of that dull but valorous cavalier and his fighting men, caused the Pathán serious misgivings. On the 15th an envoy from Sindhia had arrived in Delhi, followed by 2000 good cavalry under Raiájí Sindhia, a member of the Patel's clan already mentioned. It became known too that the Patel had written to Begam Sumroo, begging her to do all in her power; she had several times shown her loyalty, and was now within four marches, with five battalions of foot, under European officers, supported further by fifty guns. It was nothing but Ismáil and his troopers that guarded Delhi on the north and west, and gave Ghulám Kádir time for his researches in the palace. He therefore sent a donative of five *lákhs* to them, and begged them to levy contributions, in a regular manner, from the Hindu bankers and traders of the city.

The Pathán, deeming himself secure, proceeded to further investigations. On the 29th he sent for the Sháh and caused him to be flogged in his presence, employing Bédar Bakht to ply the scourge on his august kinsman's back. Next day a wholesale flogging of the Imperial Princesses took place, and their shrill laments rang through the glorious galleries of Sháh Jahán. On the 1st of August a pressing attempt was made to shake the constancy of the Sháh and extort from him the key of a secret which had, in fact, no existence. The Sháh employed the strongest forms of denial: 'If,' said he, 'you suppose that I have concealed any treasure it must be in my own body. Rip me up and see.' The tormentor then tried the effect of fair words and promises; but they were equally vain, as a matter of necessity. 'God protect you; He has laid me aside,' said the poor old man: 'I am contented with my fate.'

When the ladies, some of them the widows of deceased sovereigns, had been stripped of their small possessions, they were driven out to starve in the streets. Determined not to have all these crimes on his conscience for nothing, the Pathán sought for money right and left. The Názir, once his friend, he squeezed of seven *lákhs*. On the 3rd he lolled upon the throne by the side of his *protégé*, Bédar Bakht, smoking a water-pipe and sending the smoke into the Prince's face. In some such moments of repose he observed that a few fragments of gold still adhered to the decorations; accordingly he gave orders for the total destruction of this venerable frame, which had survived the devastations of Nádir Sháh; and had all the bullion collected and thrown into the melting-pot. On the 7th he had a fit of remorse, during which he paid the old Emperor a visit, and offered to place on the throne his favourite son Akbar. That prince, curiously enough, did succeed, years later; and it was his son who was titular ruler for five months in 1857, when he permitted, if he did not order, worse atrocities than what he had witnessed as a child.

At last, on the 10th of August, Ghulám Kádir found that he could command but little more time, and his small stock of patience was consumed by the twofold inroads of a crazy temper and a sense of coming danger[1]. Followed by some of the more ruffianly of his men he entered the *Diwán Khás*, and ordered that the deposed Sháh should be brought before him. Once more the secret treasure was demanded, and once more the existence of treasure and of a secret was denied. After some further taunting and torturing of his children, the old man was thrown; his eyes were cut out by the knives of the Patháns; and the same fate would have been dealt to all the Princes present, old and young, but for the humane expostulations of the Treasurer, whom the Pathán did not care to offend.

The luckless Sháh was then dragged off to the part of the palace reserved for deposed Emperors and other such illustrious captives; and Ghulám Kádir had leisure for the indulgence of remorse and for a serious

[1] In moments of depression he attempted to excuse himself to his followers by saying that he was acting by angelic inspiration.

consideration of his position. On the 12th he made a fresh attempt to conciliate Ismáil Beg; but that Mughal Murat was in no mood to be attached to such a cause. On the 14th, bodies of Maráthá troops began to appear in the country, south of the city, sent from Mathura by Sindhia; and Ismáil Beg began to negotiate with emissaries from Rána Khán, Sindhia's favourite 'Brother' and General. The city was all but invested; the shop-keepers had shut up their shops and fled; scarcity prevailed, intensifying day by day. Persons of the most illustrious birth died of famine in the palace; the spoiler alone continued to revel and banquet.

But his men would not starve; and they now demanded provisions with murmurs and threats. One mutiny at least broke out, which the Pathán only suppressed at the risk of his life. On the 7th of September he resolved to abandon his position, now growing untenable; he sent all his men across the river to the camp at Sháhdara—the only spot of which he retained command, for Ismáil had now ceased to give any support to an associate so useless and so discreditable. The bulk of the plunder was despatched towards Ghausgarh, a strong place near Muzafarnagar, of which nothing but the mosque now remains. On the 14th, Ghulám Kádir made a last attempt to extort from Sháh 'Alam the supposed secret of the hid treasure.

This curious situation was prolonged for more than three weeks, during which neither party cared to attack the other. At length came the 11th of October, the last day of the great Musalmán Fast of *Muharam*: and it became known that Ismáil Beg had joined Rána Khán who had also received reinforcements from the Deccan. Ghulám Kádir perceived that inaction was no longer possible. At any moment his camp might be attacked or the palace fortifications stormed. At nightfall, therefore, he blew up the powder magazine of the 'Red Castle'—so the palace is called—and hurried across the river on an elephant, sending before him a number of hostages, consisting of members of the royal family, including Bédar Bakht, his own titular sovereign.

Rána Khán immediately took possession of the palace, and caused the conflagration to be extinguished which was spreading from the magazine. Sháh 'Alam and the remaining ladies of his family were set at liberty, consoled, and provided with necessaries and comforts. The General then sent to Sindhia a report and a request for reinforcements, while the Patháns broke up from Sháhdara and began their retreat northward.

It will be observed that the Darbár of Poona had been continuously supporting and strengthening the Patel. We have already had to mention three supplies of troops sent to him during his recent difficulties. The last was commanded by Takúji Holkar; and it may be taken as a proof of Sindhia's moral influence and of the confidence which he inspired that this was so. After due preliminary arrangements, as to division of labour and of the prospective prize, the combined force set off in pursuit of the Patháns. The latter, loaded with booty, had not been able to march farther than Mirath (now, as 'Meerut,' a well-known British Cantonment). Here, in those days, was a large fort into which Ghulám Kádir entered with the flower of his force, hoping for support from some of the Rohillá Chiefs of the neighbourhood and, perhaps, from the Cis-Sutlej Sikhs. Villain as he was, perhaps a criminal lunatic, Ghulám Kádir did not want for courage or for conduct; but Sindhia felt that the wolf was now trapped, and caused the siege to be hotly pressed. The fort was completely invested, provisions failed, and after an obstinate defence of two months' duration Ghulám Kádir offered terms of surrender. These being refused, a general assault was delivered on 21st December. The garrison defended the walls through the short winter day; but their Chief found that there was no more to be expected from followers who were weary of his ill-success if not disgusted by his crimes. He therefore mounted his horse at nightfall and escaped by a sally-port, with the more portable part of his booty concealed in the stuffing of his saddle. In the morning the garrison surrendered; the disappointment of Sindhia's officers may be imagined. But it was not destined to endure. The fugitive was brought in by the peasantry of the neighbourhood, by whom he had been seized and bound. Rána Khán immediately ordered a strong escort to convey him to the presence of Sindhia at Mathura, where exemplary punishment would doubtless have been awarded. But the indignant soldiers spared their master all trouble: insulted and ill-treated on the road Ghulám Kádir was unable to control his temper: he became violent, and the men first blinded him, then mutilated, and finally hanged him on a road-side tree, 3rd of March, 1789. The scene of this punishment is traditionally said to have been at Farrah, half-way between Agra and Mathura; and Sindhia could do no more than send the mangled trunk to Delhi, where it was laid before the sightless Emperor, the most ghastly offering that was ever presented in the beautiful *Diwán Khás*[1]. The town of Ghausgarh was entirely destroyed with the exception of the great mosque. Bédar Bakht was made a prisoner and the Názir trampled to death by an elephant.

Turning from these tragic scenes, we observe, with a sense of relief, the generous efforts of Sindhia to provide for his unfortunate sovereign. By the unwritten canons of Islám, no blind man could be a Sultan; but Sindhia meant to do the whole business of State in future, and to spare the Sháh the pain of a formal deposition. The Emperor was enthroned with due pomp, and the homage of the Peshwá and his Deputy was duly presented. Writing less than

[1] This is the pillared hall, still glowing with arabesque, on the cornice of which are painted the lines, 'If there be a heaven on earth It is this, it is this, it is this.' The scenes that have taken place there have been often such as to be more suggestive of another place.

two years later, M. de Boigne declared that Sháh 'Alam was still revered as the source of power and the fountain of honour in the entire peninsula, and expressly asserted that 'Sindhia participated in the reverence.' A civil list of nine *lákhs* (say £90,000) a year was settled for the support of the Crown, to which the British Government, though resolutely withholding tribute, added a compassionate allowance[1]. The Emperor was also allowed to appropriate the complimentary offerings of those who desired to be presented. For two generations more this faded semblance of a once mighty Empire continued to be maintained; and the East India Company coined money in the name of the Emperor long after its servants had become the paramount power in India. In 1815, Lord Moira refused to visit Delhi because the then occupant of the palace, Sháh 'Alam's son and successor, would not receive him on an equal footing. Criers still made public notices with the exordium—'The country is the Sháh's; the power is the Company's; the people is God's.' The tenacity of the feeling was shown in 1857, when the revolted Sepoys ruined their chances by collecting round Sháh 'Alam's grandson. When Delhi was taken the aged representative of the House of Taimur was taken to Burma, where he and his heir died in

[1] After the campaign of 1803 a monthly allowance of 90,000 *Sicca* rupees was settled by Lord Wellesley on Sháh 'Alam and his family, amounting to something considerably over £110,000 a year, exclusive of landed estates.

captivity and exile; the collateral members have merged in the general population.

It would therefore be an injustice and a mistake to consider Sindhia as the destroyer of the Empire. In very difficult circumstances he failed to support and protect an imbecile sovereign who was intriguing against him and playing into the hands of his opponents. Perhaps he might have prevented the deplorable events which occurred in the palace during the summer of 1788; but he had better means of judging possibilities than we can have: he could not have foreseen the conduct of a crazy ruffian who was then only known as a distinguished nobleman of ability and courage: and when at last he did interfere it cost him great reinforcements and a serious effort. But, when these had been crowned by a tardy success, he then displayed his usual good sense by saving from the wreck such shreds of empire as could be saved, and by maintaining forms respected by the public even while keeping the reality of power for his own use.

CHAPTER VII

SINDHIA AND GENERAL DE BOIGNE

SHÁH 'ALAM was an author, and wrote Persian poetry under the alias of Aftáb ('Sun'). A curious specimen of his work has been preserved, a sort of Psalm composed after he had been blinded by Ghulám Kádir; and a short extract may serve to show the change that had come over his sentiments in respect to the subject of this memoir after the failure of his hope of a Muhammadan revival.

> 'Now that this young Afghán has destroyed the dignity of my State,
> I see none but Thee, O Most High! to have pity on me:
> Yet peradventure Timur Sháh, my kinsman, may come to my aid,
> And Mádhuji Sindhia—who is as a son to me—will avenge my cause:
> Ásaf-ud-daula also; and the chiefs of the English,
> They too may come to my relief:
> Shame were it if princes and peoples gathered not together,
> To the end that they might bring me help!'

Here we have a glimpse of sound judgment and cheerful hope. The fallen monarch sees at last who are his true friends. Timur Sháh, son of the famous

Daurâni of Pánípat, had married the Sháh's daughter; and perhaps aid from that quarter might have proved a source of ultimate embarrassment. But the others were all such as to give real help; Ásaf-ud-daulá was the Nawáb of Oudh, who had always shown an interest, however languid, in the Empire of which he was, in title, the hereditary Prime Minister. The like may be said of the 'English,' or rather British Government in Bengal, which professed to hold the eastern provinces under the Sháh's commission. As for Sindhia, he is now the Sháh's chief hope; and, instead of being blamed for neglect, is spoken of as 'a son.' The hope, in his case, was not entirely vain; and Sindhia was not wanting in filial attentions.

He still, however, adhered to his favourite idea of being only a village-dignitary, acting as a subordinate agent of the Peshwá who was the real Vicegerent of the Mughal Empire. Accordingly, in native parlance, he is always known by the strange and discordant epithet of 'Máháraja Patel'; or, as we might say, His Highness the Mayor. By the Emperor, however, he was now decorated with the more sonorous titles of *Madár-ul-mahám, Ali Jáh, Bahádur*.—'Exalted and illustrious Centre of affairs'; and, if a Mayor at all, he was Mayor-of-the-palace.

His position was greatly improved by the recent revolution. In Muhammad Beg and Ghulám Kádir he had two formidable heads of Musalmán opposition, both of whom had been swept from his path. Ismáil Beg still remained; but he was for the present gained to the side of order, having been conciliated by Rána Khán: Sindhia presently found a farther means of attaching the brave but unintelligent *sabreur* by bestowing on him a part of the fief of Najaf Kuli who had lately died. The estates of this Chief were in the Rewári country, between Delhi and Alwar, and were the subject of counter-claims on the part of the Mewátis and the Játs; so that Ismáil not only had the honour of being an imperial feudatory, but also a prospect of occupation which would keep him out of mischief. Doubtless, if the Afgháns should return and attempt a new crescentade, there was no certainty that Ismáil would have the self-control to keep out of the fray. We have ventured already to call this Chief 'the Mughal Murat'; he resembled the unlucky King of Naples in more ways than one, and one point of likeness was that he could not be trusted to act consistently, or with common prudence.

Another present difficulty was the want of European officers. Médoc had returned to France, where he was killed in a duel. De Boigne was dealing in indigo at Lucknow; and the officer who had taken his place had suddenly disappeared, having, as was supposed, caught the jewel-bearing charger of Ghulám Kádir when that Chief was captured by the Mirath villagers[1]. The Patel was more than ever convinced

[1] His name appears to have been Listeneaux; and the crown-jewels which he was believed to have appropriated have never been heard of since.

of the great importance of regular infantry and field-batteries under European discipline and leading: he accordingly determined, most wisely from this point of view, to ask M. de Boigne to return on his own terms. The Duke of Wellington, in later years, expressed, from another point of view, doubts as to the wisdom of this course, stating the opinion that the Maráthás would have 'been more formidable if they had never had a European or an infantry soldier in their service[1].' But that opinion must be taken with the surrounding circumstances. As opposed to Asiatic troops, disciplined and led in the mediaeval manner, any tincture of scientific warfare was advantageous. Proofs of this have already appeared; they will become more frequent presently.

M. de Boigne was one of the most upright and able soldiers then in India, and by no means a man to shrink from hard work. But he had learned the art of war in good schools—in the Irish brigade that fought at Fontenoy, in the army of Catherine II against the Turks, and in the native army of the Company at Madras in the very stress of the first Mysore War. He therefore knew the principles of scientific warfare, and he had learned how to apply them to the people and conditions of India. But to command two battalions and a light field-battery, however well-disciplined, was a thankless task when your leader was a promoted waterman or a self-taught Maráthá, whose natural

[1] *Selections from Correspondence*, Sidney Owen, p. 336.

resources were a bamboo spear and a clean pair of heels.

Nevertheless, to be himself a General, to organise and lead a uniform body, with complete solidarity and complete independence of other forces—this was what had been de Boigne's ambition ever since he left Calcutta; and he had only withdrawn his services and taken to other paths when he found that he was expected to remain subordinate to incapable leaders and to be exposed to danger and responsibility by other men's blunders.

Sindhia, for his part, was in no humour to make impossible terms. In addition to the difficulties already mentioned, his regulars were now in mutiny. Their Colonel had deserted, leaving eight months' pay in arrears; and that is what the most disciplined mercenaries will not endure: Sindhia, on the other hand, would not brook mutiny, however it might be justified. An accommodation was effected with de Boigne, who was made commandant with discretionary powers. He prevailed upon Sindhia to abstain from his original plan of charging the battalions with all his cavalry, undertaking that they should be duly dealt with. He then, by a mixture of open threats and secret hints of pardon, prevailed on them to pile their arms and parade without them; the battalions were then formally disbanded, after which the new commander re-enlisted all the men on new terms, with a present payment of half the arrears due; but he cashiered the officers who had been guilty of fomenting the discontents. Recruits were then sought for in Rohilkhand and Oudh—the future nursery of the famous Bengal army that committed suicide in 1857. The non-commissioned officers of the augmented force were taken from the best of the old battalions. By this scheme a show of punishment was inflicted for what had not been a very malicious offence; and precious material was utilised for future service.

The new force which, with Sindhia's willing consent, was now organised, gradually attained the strength of three brigades; each of which, again, consisted of eight battalions; some Mughal horse and forty field-pieces: each battalion had a European commandant, with some European or half-breed captains. The General was at first allowed 4000 Rs. a month, afterwards increased to 6000; and he was soon after allotted certain revenue-paying districts about Alígarh from whence to provide the pay of his men and the expenses of his small army: the said districts being under his own direct management. This arrangement is a good example of the system of *jaigirs* (or *tankhwáh-jaidád*, as the technical phrase went), and will be found more fully described hereafter.

By dint of unremitting labour the force was got into a semblance of readiness early in 1790, though it must have wanted hammering on the anvil of discipline, to say nothing of the hardening temper of war. Still, as compared with the rest of the army, de Boigne's corps was as the steel head was to the bamboo lance; and an opportunity soon offered for testing the weapon in active conflict. It has already been seen how unsteady were the motives and actions of Ismáil Beg, and how little Sindhia could reckon either on his judgment or his fidelity. We have also observed the hostility of the Rájput Chiefs towards Sindhia. They had lately been in a state of sullen acquiescence; but had now recovered their spirits for another campaign; and the Beg, who regarded such things in the light of pleasure-parties, willingly left his dull life in Mewát, and took the field as an ally of Jaipur and Jodhpur pending the hoped-for descent of Taimur Sháh from Kábul and Ghazní.

To confront this combination, Sindhia sent forth a grand expedition under Gopál Ráo Bháo, and Lakwá Dáda, famous for his defence of Agra. To this was attached the new corps of General de Boigne, and they marched towards Jaipur in the hope of anticipating the junction between the Beg and his Rájput allies. The Beg was hurrying towards the rendezvous at the head of a body of men-at-arms, disbanded Afgháns and Persians, who had flocked to him in answer to his first summons.

In speaking of these men as 'cuirassiers' and 'men-at-arms' an attempt is made to indicate that what was now devolving upon Sindhia was the experiment of opposing modern war to mediaeval war, men with muskets to men in armour. A detailed account of the battle of Pánípat was given in Chapter II, partly in order to show that the young Maráthá had then seen the experiment tried for the first time and ended by the most complete failure. The mailed horsemen of the Durání had utterly destroyed the southern army in spite of the gallant efforts of Ibráhím Gárdi. It must therefore strike us as a strong mark of clearness and originality that Sindhia should have been able to pick the truth from such a confusing medium, and see that Ibráhím's overthrow proved nothing against the system. The 'Gárdis' had completely baffled the Persian cavalry at Pánípat; and had all the Maráthá infantry been like them, the result would have been the same all along the line. Sindhia might, we say, have observed this, with his clear vision; he certainly saw it in Goddard's campaign in 1779; and perhaps, in later days, Gen. de Boigne may have quoted to him the remark made by Bernier in the palmy days of the Empire, that 'twenty-five thousand good troops under Turenne or Condé would trample under foot all the hosts of the Great Mughal.'

That, then, was the issue now to be submitted to the arbitrament of actual warfare. Sindhia despatched his army from Mathura in March, 1790; de Boigne, though not ostensibly Commander-in-Chief, appears to have assumed direction as soon as the seat of war was reached. Early in May the army passed by Gwalior, and a cloud of light Maráthá cavalry was sent out to cover the further advance and obtain intelligence of the enemy. On the 10th they sent word that Ismáil was intrenched at Pátan, in the rocky country between

Gwalior and Ajmere, not very far from the scene of the three days' battle of 1787, at Lálsot. The Rájputs were at hand; and the dreaded junction might have been easily effected. How dangerous these men were was afterwards to be shown. Indolent and untrained, they had habits of the most utter devotion; especially was this the case with the Ráthor cavaliers of Jodhpur, a body of whom, some years later, rode down du Drenec's brigade of regular troops, under French officers, in spite of a loss of 1500 of their number rolled over by grape from the well-served field-pieces[1]. But on the present occasion the raw levies of de Boigne were saved from this experience. The vigilance of Sindhia had been on the alert; presents and promises had been made; and the support of these gallant Hindus was withheld from the Muhammadan adventurers. Left to his own resources, the Beg for more than three weeks defended his lines against the assaults of the Maráthás. At last, his scanty stock of patience being quite exhausted, provisions also probably falling short, he sallied out, to assume the offensive, on the 19th of June. The Mughal men-at-arms, with trumpets and kettle-drums, and flashing armour, thundered down upon de Boigne's field-batteries and sabred the gunners at their posts. Between the charges the infantry were pelted by grape from the intrenchments, and de Boigne had

[1] This battle was fought at Sanganir in 1799: Skinner has described it from his own observation. In spite of the gallantry of their cavalry the Rájputs lost the day.

to form square, like Wellington just a quarter of a century later, as fast as the hostile horsemen renewed their charges. Towards the end of the day de Boigne, observing signs of exhaustion on the part of the enemy, determined upon reversing the situation. Placing himself in front of the line he deployed his unbroken battalions and led them against the batteries. The first was carried with the shock; a hard struggle took place for the second, but it was mastered by 8 p.m.; the third fell an hour after; the enemy ceased to resist, and their leader with his personal following fled for refuge to the city of Jaipur. The abstinence of Holkar, who was near enough to have taken the part of Blücher in 1815, rendered the pursuit imperfect; nevertheless Ismáil lost his guns, elephants, and baggage; and on the following day his regular battalions and ten thousand irregular troops went over to the Maráthás. De Boigne in his report estimates the Mughal cavalry at 5000 sabres; and attributes his success to the firmness of his own battalions. 'Thank God,' he adds, 'I have realised all the sanguine expectations of Sindhia.' How steadily his men must have fought may be judged from their return of 120 killed and 472 wounded. The aggregate forces of the enemy were estimated at 20,000 horse and 25,000 foot, with one hundred pieces of artillery; the whole of which, however, did not come into action; those who did were worsted by the steady valour of less than 10,000 men, mostly young soldiers who had never seen a shot fired in anger.

In not giving substantial aid to the Beg, Partáb Singh may seem to have acted a spiritless part. But the Kachwáha tribe, of which he was the head, were a more peaceful people, and lived in more accessible places than their Rájput brethren of Márwar or Jodhpur. Old Bijai Singh, the Jodhpur Rájá, finally succumbed to Sindhia's superior forces; but he had not made up his mind to do so without another struggle, which he began by a clumsy attempt to corrupt Gen. de Boigne, in his eyes no better than the ordinary military adventurer of the India of that day. He accordingly sent a message to the General in which, after many compliments upon his late exhibition of skill and valour, he was proffered the gift of the town of Ajmere and the surrounding district on condition of his joining the Rájputs against Sindhia. But the General answered, with polite but grim pleasantry, that Sindhia had already bestowed upon him not only Ajmere but all the territories of Jaipur and Jodhpur; so that his respected correspondent might judge of the insufficiency of the tendered bribe. On the 21st of August, 1790, the General proceeded to make good his boast by entering the town of Ajmere, which was not sufficiently strong, either in fortification or garrison, to offer the faintest resistance.

This famous town is the centre of a plateau forming the watershed of the part of India in which its boundaries lie, and it is the highest point on the plains of Hindustán. It is bounded on the north by the States of Kishngarh and Jodhpur, on the west by Jodhpur, on the south by Udaipur, and on the east by Kishangarh and the Jaipur territory: and it is crossed by the chain of the Arávalli Hills, of which the highest peak—2855 feet above sea-level—is occupied by the citadel, which is called Táragarh (Star-Fort), a solid work of the Jodhpur Rájás dating from the days of Bábar, founder of the Mughal Empire. Taken by the Emperor Akbar, who built a palace by the lake and surrounded the city with stone walls, the city formed a place of arms; and during the vigorous period of the Empire it continued to be an occasional country-seat of the sovereign and a strategic point for the command and control of the surrounding principalities of the Rájputs. In the decadence under Muhammad Sháh, it was taken, for Bijai Singh, by Jai Apa, a chief of the Sindhia clan; but Bijai Singh soon after murdered Jai Apa and occupied the place on his own account. In 1754 he was attacked by Malhár Ráo and Jánkluji Sindhia (Madhu's grandfather) by whom he was compelled to acknowledge the overlordship of the Maráthá power, and was allowed to hold the city and districts as a vassal of that State. When Jaipur and Jodhpur rose against Sindhia in 1787, as related in Chapter IV, the Ráthors of the latter State annulled their tributary engagement; and it had now become a paramount object with Sindhia to recover the position, by which he would not only give the Rájputs a signal lesson but would regain a post which severed their communications with each other. It was for these reasons that he had, as General de Boigne put it, given Ajmere to him.

The fort of Táragarh commands the town, and is almost entirely surrounded by precipices which it seems impossible to scale. Elsewhere the approach is defended by walls more than three yards in thickness and twenty feet high, built of huge blocks of stone hewn and fitted. In the enclosure are large tanks of rain-water, which furnish an almost inexhaustible supply[1]. Despite these advantages it now seemed in danger of yielding to the skill and audacity of the General and his 'new model' before the tardy Ráthors could arrive for its relief.

Informed of their approach, the General turned from his prey and, leaving 2700 men to maintain the blockade of Táragarh, he marched down the Jodhpur road. He found the Ráthors encamped under the protection of the walls of Merta, seventy-six miles north-east of Ajmere. The spot was of evil omen for Bijai Singh, being the very scene of his defeat by Sindhia's uncle thirty-six years before. On the evening of the 9th of September de Boigne came in sight of the Ráthor position, which was on a level plain protected on the rear by the town, situated on a rising ground and fortified partly with earthen mounds, partly by walls of masonry. De Boigne's colleague, Gopál Ráo, urged him to attack without delay; but the General's superior caution and science overcame the ardour of the Maráthá. The men, as

[1] See *Imperial Gazetteer, in v.* Ajmere-Merwárá.

he observed, had made a long march, and stood in need of food and rest; while, should they, as was to be hoped, defeat the enemy, the approaching darkness would render pursuit impossible. The Maráthá yielding to these arguments, arrangements were made for the night, and for a general attack before daybreak. On the other side the enemy passed the night in festivity. In point of numbers the two armies were not very unequal: if the Ráthors were superior in cavalry the troops of Sindhia were better disciplined and equipped; the Ráthor horse were estimated at 30,000 sabres; but they were not so strong in infantry or, indeed, in generalship.

In the grey of the morning, while the old Rájá and his men were sleeping off their debauch, their camp was surprised by Col. de Rohan at the head of three of de Boigne's best battalions. But the surprise was momentary. A body of Ráthor cavalry, of the famous Chándawat clan, rapidly formed and mounted, drove out Rohan's battalions, and charged down upon the Maráthá horsemen of the right wing. Scattering these like chaff before the wind, the gallant cavaliers re-formed to ride back. But the infantry had recovered from their confusion: in serried squares bristling with bayonets and dealing out a well-nourished fire, they barred the way; field-pieces vomited grape from the intervals; the story goes that four thousand saddles were emptied in the return ride. Relieved from this tempest, the battalions of de Boigne deployed into line and advanced upon the Ráthor camp, supported by their field-batteries. The Ráthors fought well till 9 o'clock; their camp was stormed by 10, and then they fled, their retreat covered by the remainder of their cavalry. The whole camp, with munitions of war and a vast plunder, fell into the hands of the conquerors; and the town was taken by assault the same afternoon.

Táragarh, left to its own resources, capitulated; and on the 18th of November Bijai Singh made his peace with his irresistible antagonist, who entered Jodhpur on that day: the Rána of Udaipur hastened to follow his example. The humble slipper-carrier was now at his zenith; he who, as the last wreck of a ruined family and a lost cause, had barely escaped with his life forty years before by the help of a humane waterman, was now lord of Central India and great part of Hindustán. But he thought nothing done while aught remained to do; and the next task that he imposed upon his able General was the punishment of Jaipur, where Ismáil Beg had been harboured after the defeat of Páthan. But the Rájá, Partáb Singh, was now isolated: Ismáil had left him, to take fresh harbour with the widow of Najaf Kuli Khán—lately deceased. Bijai Singh and other Chiefs of the Rájputs had been beaten into submission; and the Jaipuris, as already stated, were not of exceptional enterprise or tenacity. After one faint attempt at resistance, which was overcome in a single battle, Partáb Singh also submitted.

In order to retain his dearly-bought supremacy,

Sindhia now determined on a further augmentation of the section of his army to which it was so evidently due. De Boigne was accordingly instructed to raise his legion to 18,000 regular infantry with a number of light troops and some additional guns: and a tract of country was assigned for the support of the forces, which extended from Delhi to Mathura, and northward to the boundary of what is now the district of Bulandshahr. The total land revenue of this tract was twenty-two *lákhs* a year; and it was reckoned that, after liquidating the pay of officers and men, the General would have for his administrative labours a recompense in the shape of a surplus profit of 40,000 Rs. a year; independent of which he drew his pay, now raised to 6000 Rs. monthly, besides miscellaneous perquisites. His headquarters were to be Alígarh, where he built a house, called Sáhib-Bágh, which is still to be seen half-way between the fort and the town of Koïl. His arsenal was in the fort of Agra.

But, before the submission of Jaipur had allowed the General to enter upon the peaceful labours of a civil administrator, he was obliged to take the field against a new and unexpected enemy.

In 1791 Lord Cornwallis found himself obliged to abandon his peaceful policy and make war upon Tipú, the Sultan of Mysore. The operations were, at first, far from successful; and Sindhia, who was always somewhat distracted between admiration for the British soldier and perplexity at the policy of the British statesman, thought that the failure of the campaign offered an opportunity which he ought not to neglect. He therefore proposed to the Governor-General an alliance in which he should take part in the operations against Tipú on condition that two British battalions should temporarily attend his person, and that he should be otherwise assisted in operations in Rájputána. Somewhat to his surprise, the proposal was courteously declined; but if the manner was friendly, the act was not the less ungracious. Sindhia's surprise deepened into alarm when he found that the Court of Poona had been applied to when his aid had been rejected; and that the Nána had pledged the Peshwá to a participation in the next campaign.

By the coalition treaty, signed on the 1st of June, 1790, the darbár of Poona had agreed to furnish 10,000 men, though the Nána did not at once recall his agent from Tipú's Court. Their assistance was the reverse of profitable to Cornwallis; but the British soon showed how little dependent they were on any Maráthá aid. In 1792 Cornwallis resumed the offensive, took one strong place after another, and sat down before Seringapatam, with a strong and thoroughly equipped army in February. Tipú was fain to submit and to cede territory yielding over one hundred *lákhs* of yearly revenue; and, despite their languid support, the Maráthás were rewarded by a third of this acquisition.

While Sindhia was being thus countermined and

isolated by the ingenious Nána, he was threatened by another peril. The terror of northern invasion, which had been so cruel a reality in living memory, was reviving. Sindhia was wont to declare that, in his dreams, he still often heard the lobbing paces of the Afghán pursuer's horse and the roar of his broken wind. A repetition of the campaign of 1760–1 seemed always possible; and it was never certain that one of its features would not be a Musalmán league in which the part of Shujá-ud-daulá would be repeated by his son, with Ismáil Beg for his champion. The Beg was still abroad, and, for the present, beyond reach; but the Nawáb was at hand, lazy and unpopular. Here again the British stopped the way. Major Palmer was instructed to inform Sindhia that, in any just claims upon Oudh, the good offices of the Government were at his service; but he was warned that the Nawáb was the ally of the British, who would resent any injury done to him or to the people of his province.

CHAPTER VIII

Sindhia in Apogee

The good news of de Boigne's successes in Ráj-putána formed some kind of compensation to Madhoji as he pondered over the circumstances of the political situation in his favourite cantonment of Mathura. This was a place of peculiar sanctity in Hindu opinion; but its chief recommendation to the judgment of Sindhia was not, perhaps, so much its sanctity as its strategic and political advantages. About half-way between his arsenal at Agra and the capital of the empire at Delhi, it commanded the Ját country and afforded easy access, by way of Gwalior, to Málwá and the Deccan. Now, when he was becoming un-easy in regard to the attitude of the British and of the Nána, he determined to leave de Boigne in charge of his interests in Hindustán and make a personal appearance at the Court of Poona.

We have already (v. Chap. II) sketched the state of things at the Maráthá capital up to the Treaty of Salbái in 1782. Since then Raghuba had been put into confinement, and Mádhava Ráo II, brother of the murdered Naráyan Ráo, had been set up as Peshwá, the control of affairs being assumed by the Nána. Malhár Ráo's son's widow having approved of this arrangement allowed her henchman, Takúji, to lead the forces of Indore, sometimes against Mysore, sometimes against Sindhia's Rájput and Musalmán enemies. Numberless instances are on record of the wisdom and benevolence of this lady—whose honoured name was Ahalya Bái—and she was a good friend to Sindhia to the end of his public life: on one occasion supplying an emergent necessity of his with a generous gift of thirty *lákhs*, disguised as a loan of which repayment was never demanded.

Ahalya Bái resided at Indore—still the capital of the Holkar dominions, a short distance south of Sindhia's Málwá capital of Ujjain; and it is believed that at no period in the history of that fertile country have the people lived in more peaceful or prosperous enjoyment of their natural advantages or had a more truly popular government than under these two benevolent and able rulers. The golden age of Málwá, in the midst of distracted neighbours, lasted thirty years after her death, the people still fondly spoke of her as an 'Avatár,' or divine incarnation. 'Ahalya Bái,' said a female contemporary, 'is not beautiful; but the light of Heaven is upon her face.'

In 1791 the Bái was growing old, being worn by incessant attention to business and by religious austerities. Takúji had always shown respect and obedience to her behests; but he was becoming jealous of Sindhia's greatness, and dissatisfied with the division of territory and revenue which had been acquired by the help of his forces, but of which Sindhia seemed to reap all the harvest. Takúji was now in Málwá, engaged in forming a rival to Sindhia's regular force: for which purpose he had retained the services of the Chevalier du Drenec, a Breton officer of experience and repute. Apart from this threatening aspect of the chief soldier of the Indore State, Sindhia had other reasons for desiring a personal influence in Poona politics. Though so much absorbed in remote affairs and interests, he had always done his best to keep touch with the Nána; and it was to this that he had been indebted, during his late reverses, for timely help, supplied at first somewhat grudgingly, but more freely at last. Now, however, the attitude of Holkar was becoming hostile and the Nána's support doubtful.

Accordingly, Sindhia made a slow and tentative march through Central India, accompanied by a small but compact force so as not to cause alarm, and announcing that he was only coming as a messenger from Sháh 'Alam, charged with presents and insignia for the young Peshwá. He arrived at Poona on the 11th of June, 1792, and pitched in the grounds of the British Residency. Ten days later, he proceeded to wait upon the Peshwá in darbár, bringing as his offering all sorts of costly rarities and products of Hindustán. The virtual sovereign ruler of Hindustán, victorious in diplomacy or war over all opponents, lord of vast provinces and of unconquered legions, he approached the State-enclosure on foot, leaving his elephant and his body-guard of grenadiers under European officers at the confines of his own camp. On entering the tent he took his station below all the officials present; when the Peshwá appeared Sindhia made his obeisance with the rest; and, declining the invitation to be seated, produced a bundle, out of which he unwrapped a pair of new slippers. 'This,' he murmured, 'was my father's occupation, and it must also be mine.' Then, reverently removing the slippers which the young Chief had been wearing, he wrapped them in the cloth from which he had taken the new pair; and, having laid them before the Peshwá, permitted himself to accept the reiterated invitation to be seated, still carrying the Peshwá's old shoes under his arm.

Next day there was a second, and even more solemn levée, for the purpose of publicly investing the Peshwá with the office of Vicegerent of the Empire and with its symbolical insignia. At the end of the principal tent stood an empty throne which represented the throne of the Emperor; and upon this the Peshwá deposited an offering of one hundred and one gold mohrs [1]. He then followed Sindhia into a side-room, whence he presently emerged, clothed in robes of honour, wearing five superb pieces of jewelry and bearing in one hand a sword, in the other a seal and inkstand. Fans of peacock's feathers and a

[1] Probably, like the modern *mohr*, pieces of sixteen rupees each.

gilt sedan-chair, a charger, and six elephants, laden with banners of state and emblems of heraldry, completed the pageant. Two patents from the Imperial Chancery were then exhibited—one allowing Sindhia the right of appointing his successor as deputy, the other forbidding the slaughter of horned cattle.

This scene, which took place on the 22nd of June, exhibits at once the art with which Sindhia attempted to impose on the imagination of others, and the firmness with which he grasped substantial advantages for himself. It did not signify a copper piece to him whether or no the hereditary President of a dissolving confederacy wore the order of the Silver Fish as Lieutenant of a moribund Empire. He may not have greatly cared whether or no the use of beef was rendered impossible to one-fifth of the population. But for the multitude such things had an importance which he judged it prudent to consider; so that the vulgar at both extremes of society might agree to let real power remain with him from whom these good things came.

It was the same with his slipper-carrying and his title of Patel; a well-informed writer testifies that 'Madhoji made himself a sovereign by calling himself a servant.' Such was the tradition when Malcolm wrote, in Málwá, a quarter of a century later[1].

Leaving Sindhia in the performance of duties which may remind us of the Baron of Bradwardine,

[1] *Central India*, i. 125.

we must resume the story of events in Hindustán during his absence. Scarcely had he crossed the Narbadá when Holkar advanced on Hindustán. Summoning Ismáil Beg from his temporary retirement, he forced a rupture with Sindhia's agents by demanding a settlement of accounts.

Ismáil was the first and nearest danger. The widow of Najaf Kuli Khán was a sister of the late Ghulám Kádir; and, like him, had inherited some of the turbulent spirit of their father, the troublesome but ineffectual Zábita Khán. She now put Ismáil Beg in command of one of her strong places, the fort of Kánaund, where her husband was residing at the time of his death, and which he had strengthened in view of the possible eventualities of those troubled times. It was a stronghold of earthen walls faced with stone, on the border of the Bikaner desert; and being surrounded by sandhills and tamarisk scrub, was unfavourable to the approach of a hostile army, seeing that it was both deficient in water-supply and almost impassable for siege-guns. De Boigne, however, saw the necessity of striking quick and hard. He therefore ordered a brigade of infantry with field-pieces to march against Kánaund, under Colonel Perron—afterwards his successor in the command of the regular troops. Perron, whom the General then considered a plain soldier, possessed of honesty and good sense, lost no time in making his way through the dry and difficult country. Nothing daunted by former defeats, the Beg sallied forth to the attack:

but it was to little purpose. He was worsted and driven into the Fort, the defence of which he, for the next few days, conducted to the best of his not too consummate ability. But the virago was presently killed by a shell or round shot from Perron's batteries; and her men, losing heart, began to regard Ismáil as a burden of whom they would do well to rid themselves. Discovering their feelings, and fearing that he might be handed over as a sacrifice, the Beg made up his mind to appeal to the humanity of the *Faringhi* colonel. Perron gladly agreed to spare his life on condition of his surrendering the place; and the redoubtable *sabreur* was sent as a prisoner to Agra, where he died some years after.

Scarcely was General de Boigne freed from this adversary when a more formidable opponent appeared upon the scene. This was Takúji Holkar in person; who, possibly instigated by his son, Jaswant Ráo, had shown ill-feeling against Lakwa Dáda, the representative of Sindhia in Hindustán, and crossed the Chambal with evidently hostile intentions. Gopál Ráo was the nearest of Sindhia's commanders, and he sent to de Boigne for aid, being in great alarm at the reports of Holkar's great force and especially of the new model under du Drenec. Of this there were four battalions, with their due complement of guns; but de Boigne hastened to meet them with such strength as he could command of what Sindhia called 'the army of the Empire': a strange epithet seeing that the force so described was paid and used by a

Maráthá and marched under the white cross of Savoy. The corps of de Boigne took the field 9000 strong; but before it encountered Holkar the General was joined by Lakwá Dáda with his Maráthá horse. Holkar had 30,000 cavalry and numerous guns, when de Boigne (20 September, 1792) came upon him at the Pass of Lakhairi, on the way from Kánaund to Ajmere.

Du Drenec was an experienced soldier, and the ground had been well chosen: the trained battalions held the crest of the pass, the low ground at the foot of which was still soaking with monsoon-flood: the sides were flanked by dense tree-jungle, and there were thirty-eight guns in position. Now, for the first time in Indian history, was the new warfare to be waged on both sides. Previous battles had been of the new against the old; this one was to be the first of a fresh series which only ended at Gujarát in 1849. No longer was a mailed *gendarmerie* to dash itself to pieces against the rocks of discipline and science; but field artillery and lines of musketry were to be moved against each other in tactical array. General de Boigne felt that the situation was critical, and acted with even more than his usual prudent valour. Ascending a neighbouring eminence he reconnoitred the position of the enemy, whose infantry he found posted as in an artificial work, supported by a strong artillery, and protected by the vast force of cavalry already mentioned. Then, descending to his own formations, he threw out 500

Rohillá horsemen under the screen of whose line he advanced his infantry with fixed bayonets over the swamp that lay between him and the pass. But it seemed as if every element of difficulty was to test his skill that day. His columns were at once exposed to a murderous fire from Holkar's batteries, to which he could at first make no sufficient reply, by reason of the speed with which he had advanced. As his batteries, slowly drawn by oxen, came within range a tumbril of ammunition was struck by a hostile shell, and exploded: the explosion spread around; in a moment ten or twelve others caught fire, and scattered noise, and smoke, and havoc. Holkar, observing the confusion thus engendered in de Boigne's ranks, hurled his horse against them from among the trees; the charge was vainly opposed by de Boigne's lighter and less numerous cavalry. But Holkar and his horsemen were unable to penetrate the opposite jungle, whither de Boigne had withdrawn his infantry, and at the word of command the seasoned veterans, protected in the covert, began to pour a ceaseless volley into the disorganised squadrons of Holkar. As soon as their advance was turned into retreat, de Boigne's Rohillá horse charged home; confusion became rout; and then the infantry, the victors of Pátan and Merta, supported by their guns, emerged from the covert to storm the pass. Du Dronec had but 1500 men with whom to hold it, but they did their best; not until almost all the officers and men had fallen did resistance cease upon the crest, which was at last possessed by de Boigne, with thirty-eight captured guns. The shattered forces of Holkar followed him across the Chambal, into Northern Málwá, where Takúji consoled himself for his defeat by harrying the country and sacking Sindhia's chief town Ujjain. De Boigne's experience of fighting was considerable; he had seen the three days of Lálsot, the rout of Chaksána, Rána Khán's hard-won victory at Fatehpur-Sikri, and the determined conflicts of Ismáil and Bijai Singh. But, of all the actions that he ever witnessed, this encounter with du Drenec's raw recruits was, so he asserted, the most obstinate. The quarrel, indeed, has been thought to have been, originally, rather of the nature of a personal wrangle over accounts than a regular war between the clans of Holkar and Sindhia. Nevertheless from henceforth Holkar was to Sindhia a thorn in the side; and the feud was to be inherited, as one Sindhia was succeeded by another, in the succession of a new and still more formidable Holkar.

Sindhia remained at Poona; and in July professed to have received 'orders' from the Court of Delhi to collect tribute from the British administration in Bengal. This, apparently, was one of Sindhia's tentative endeavours to ascertain how far the pacific policy of Lord Cornwallis would carry him in concession. The last attempt of that kind had been the somewhat arrogantly declined offer of alliance at the commencement of the Mysore war: and it is difficult to understand why a fresh experiment on British patience should have been attempted just as Cornwallis had brought that war to a successful termination. Nevertheless, such was the fact; and the issue of the said 'orders' was announced in the *Court Circular* of Delhi, in July 1792. A similar move had been, it may be recollected, most sternly rebuked by Macpherson's Government so far back as 1785; and the present attempt fared no better. Whether from prudence or from pride, Cornwallis would not submit to what his predecessor had already characterised as an insult. In a State-paper of 2 August, Lord Cornwallis treated the subject with all due gravity; giving orders that information should be 'conveyed to Madhoji Sindhia that—in the present condition of affairs at the Court of Delhi—he, Sindhia, would be held personally answerable for every writing that might be issued in the name of the Emperor, and that any such attempt to assert a claim to tribute from the Bengal Government would be warmly resented.' Once more the disinclination of the British to interfere in Hindustán was stated with, perhaps, superfluous emphasis, especially when one recollects what took place little more than ten years later. But a significant clause was added, to the effect that, 'should any one be rash enough to insult them by an unjust demand, in whatever shape or form, they felt themselves both disposed to resent it and fully capable of exacting satisfaction.' Whatever may be thought of the justice or legality of this attitude its effect on the clear-headed statesman for whose behoof it was displayed was ample justification of its peremptory style. Sindhia hastened to disavow the intentions attributed to him by the Delhi scribe. He assured the Governor-General that he regarded His Excellency as supreme in his own dominions, and that, for his own part, his sole object was to extend and conserve the Imperial authority in those parts of India which still remained subject to the Emperor.

How far this language was sincere must be estimated by each of us according to his own information and his own habits of thought. A brilliant Indian historian of our own day has given a picture of Sindhia's policy somewhat different from that which has been adopted in the present pages. The troops organised and disciplined by de Boigne had disposed of the Musalmán and Hindu opponents of Sindhia; 'but,' says Colonel Malleson, 'he still looked for more at their hands. It must never be lost sight of that the great dream of Mádhaji (*sic*) Sindhia's life was to unite all the native powers of India in one great confederacy against the English. In this respect he was the most far-sighted statesman that India has ever produced. . . . It was a grand idea, capable of realisation by Mádhaji, but by him alone, and which, but for his death, would have been realised [1].'

Doubtless, such a scheme would have been a 'grand'

[1] See *Final French Struggles in India*; a book in which an almost forgotten episode of Indian history is set forth in a bright and fascinating manner, and generous record given to the doings of some very gallant, though mostly unsuccessful, men.

one, if only the means for its accomplishment had been forthcoming: and we have no positive evidence that Sindhia was blind to its attractions. But those who have observed the sayings and doings of the subject of this sketch will, surely, fail to find in it any positive evidence that Sindhia had seriously entertained such a 'dream,' at any moment subsequent to the Treaty of Salbái; much less that he considered himself able to have 'realised' it. He had a great and always-growing respect for the military resources of the British, which he had seen rise superior to every power in the peninsula, whether European or Asiatic. He had twice disclaimed with almost abject apology all intention of demanding from the British Government payment of tribute, which was indeed due on the twofold ground of constitutional usage and actual treaty-obligation. He had tendered aid against Mysore when Tipú was in the plenitude of his power. He had certainly not been encouraged by General de Boigne to think that his Hindustáni levies with their two or three European, or Eurasian, officers to each battalion, could be a match against Sepoy-divisions fully provided with white officers, and stiffened with regiments of British grenadiers, and gunners, and dragoons. It is on record that his successor, on parting from de Boigne, received from that great soldier the earnest warning 'Never to quarrel with the British, and rather to disband his army than hazard it in a conflict with them.' We may safely dismiss from our minds the suspicion that

Mádhava Sindhia commissioned General de Boigne to raise or maintain his disciplined army-corps with any other intention than the obvious and avowed one of being able to 'extend and preserve the authority of the Emperor (i. e. of himself), in those territories which still remained under the direct administration of the Empire.'

After his successes against Holkar, de Boigne extorted from the vanquished and isolated Rájá of Jaipur a promise of tribute, with an immediate payment of seventy *lákhs* of rupees as a war-indemnity. He then set his face homeward, seeking repose for his men and for himself after their long and arduous labours. The character and conduct of the General are of interest to us here, as showing the acuteness which had led Sindhia to select him for employment in the first instance; and, having done so, to yield him the most implicit confidence. The after-relations between Sindhia's successor and Perron suffice to show the difficulties that beset ordinary men in such a position, and the dangers to which Sindhia and de Boigne might, like their successors, have succumbed if they had not both been men far above the ordinary level.

At the time of which we are now taking note, Perron was no more than a subordinate, carrying out with praiseworthy punctuality the orders of his superiors. When de Boigne went back to Alígarh he detached Perron, under Sindhia's orders, bidding him attend Sindhia at Poona with 10,000 of the regular infantry. In issuing these orders, Colonel Malleson conceives Sindhia to have been actuated by a desire to 'attain what had been the dream of his later years . . . to form one vast combination against the English.' In the absence of proof, we may content ourselves with supposing the plain and sufficient motive of finding material support in establishing and maintaining the preponderant influence at the Court of the young Peshwá, which was necessary to protect Sindhia against the growing hostility of the Holkars and the Nána Farnavis.

In all his acknowledged projects Sindhia had at last become perfectly successful. The fame of his political sagacity and the terror of his General's military skill and resolution were now acknowledged from the boundary of the Punjáb to the frontier of Rohilkhand from the Jumna to the Narbadá. The Chevalier du Drenec ultimately left the service of Holkar and had accepted the command of a brigade under Perron. His house is still pointed out at Koïl, where we may imagine him settled as a neighbour to Perron at *Sahib-bágh*, giving his General the benefit of his assistance and the pleasure derivable from the society of a well-bred Frenchman in the intercourse of private life. Not far off, at Sirdhana, were the headquarters of the able and ambitious Christian lady who had succeeded to the command of Sombre's brigade and to the civil management of his *jaigir*.

Indian administration was not then either understood or organised as has since been the case. A few years afterwards, when the country had been for some time under the negligent rule of Perron, the people had relapsed into a state of misery and misgovernment almost as intolerable as in the great anarchy which had followed on the invasion of Nádir Sháh, and of which a brief notice, from native sources, has been already given. The effete remains of Akbar's system had long since quite broken down; the fields were almost absorbed in forest and turned into tiger-haunted jungles. Hardly more than half a century ago one of Lord Auckland's aides-de-camp hunted tigers in the district of Muzafarnagar, where such an animal would now be as great a wonder as on Salisbury Plain. In the neglected villages the peasantry, reduced in numbers and inured to violence, withheld the payment of rent and revenue, and enhanced the scanty produce of their few cultivated acres by robbing travellers and by lifting the cattle of more prosperous neighbours. In the heart of this unhappy country de Boigne and the Begam of Sirdhana attempted the first restoration of order and welfare. The tracts assigned to the former consisted of thirty-two *parganás,* or fiscal unions, and were estimated to yield a yearly revenue of some two hundred and fifty *lákhs.* The domain of the Begam was less extensive, but the system adopted in each was very much the same.

In his civil administration the General instituted two departments; the 'Persian' side was conducted by native writers and accountants; but there was also a 'French' office under his own superintendence. The public dues were fixed by a rough assessment of the landed estates; and the collections were realised with punctuality, being enforced by the presence of the military establishments which were peremptorily employed on occasions of recalcitrance. We have no particulars of the administration of justice under de Boigne; but in later days, under Perron, it is known to have been considered of secondary importance; no regular system of law was recognised, nor were there any courts for holding proper trials; reports of inquiries by native magistrates were sent to the General, who gave the final decision, awarding punishments according to his discretion. But de Boigne was probably a safer arbitrator, as he was a far abler man. His industry was enormous. He rose, as we are told by a European witness, with dawn; surveyed his stores and factories, inspected his troops, transacted the civil business of his division, gave audience, received the reports of the criminal and fiscal officers, carried on diplomatic correspondence, and even found time to attend to his own private business. All this is perfectly conceivable when the chief is a man of method, who knows what to do himself and what to leave to subordinates, and to apply the controlling touch and maintain the motive power of the administrative machine. The Begam at Sirdhana was equally industrious and not less successful.

Another Christian ruler of almost equal ability,

just coming into a brief prominence, was the famous George Thomas, who had once held a command under the Begam, but was now carving out a principality for himself out of the fiefs of the late Najaf Kuli to the south-west of the metropolis.

While an approach to tranquillity was thus being restored to Hindustán, Sindhia remained at Poona, surrounded by his trained battalions and European satellites, endeavouring to acquire a position in the Deccan commensurate with his power in Hindustán; but he found the situation there one of much greater difficulty.

Though not directly bearing on the story, the impression produced upon a British observer by General de Boigne's career may deserve to be here recorded. 'It was not the least of the advantages arising from General de Boigne's merit that, in his military capacity, he should have softened, by means of an admirable perseverance, the ferocious and almost savage character of the Maráthás. He submitted, to the discipline and to the civilisation of European armies, soldiers who till then had been regarded as barbarians; and to such an extent did he succeed that the rapacious licence which had formerly been common amongst them came at last to be looked upon as infamous even by the meanest soldier' (*Bengal Journal* of the 18th of September, 1790). For this extract I am indebted to Colonel Malleson's interesting work already quoted. The gallant author well adds that:—

'It was de Boigne who made it possible for Sindia (*sic*) to rule in Hindostan (*sic*) at the same time that he controlled the councils of Poona. . . . It was de Boigne who introduced into the North-West Provinces the germs of that civil administration which the English have since successfully developed' (*Final French Struggles*, p. 189). The General retired to Europe soon after the death of Mádhava, probably prescient of future trouble under his less experienced and less competent successor. He died at Chambéri, 1st of June, 1830, possessed of great wealth, of which he made a noble use.

CHAPTER IX

LAST DAYS, DEATH, AND CHARACTER

THE goals at which able men desire to arrive are often reached. The true disappointment of life is that, when reached, they are found to conceal behind them something sinister and unexpected. So long as Sindhia had remained in Hindustán he might have seemed to have attained the object of his life's labour. He had become to the Emperor what the Peshwá was to the descendant of Siváji, who still wielded a toy-sceptre at Satára, and whose fiat was still necessary to fill a vacancy on the throne at Poona. Sháh 'Alam still wore the crown of Akbar in the palace of Sháh Jahán; but he was a blind septuagenarian with no voice in the disposal of events beyond the palace walls [1]. Elsewhere the affairs of peace and of war obeyed the orders of Sindhia, from the Sutlej to the Narbadá. Yet all was insecure so long as the Deccan was closed to his influence and the Nána could move the young Peshwá to issue orders that were obeyed by Holkar.

The Peshwá was Sindhia's namesake, Mádhava

[1] So late as 1789 Sháh 'Alam put to death his kinsman Bédar Bakht whom Ghulám Kádir had put on his throne.

Ráo; the same whose birth had disconcerted the schemes of Raghuba in 1773. It may be remembered that his mother was the widow of one of two brothers who had succeeded each other in the Peshwáship and disappeared in a manner so favourable to the interests of their uncle, Raghuba; who then, with the support of Governor Hornby of Bombay, assumed the office. The Nána was the widow's lover; and when her son was born, after her husband's death, and in a manner so opportune for the opponents of Raghuba, we cannot wonder if doubts were expressed as to the child's paternity. So the young Chief grew up, the subject of suspicion, the tool of faction, and with no will but to obey the will of an intriguer. He had now grown to man's estate, and bore a semblance of sovereignty; but his subsequent tragic fate serves to throw a lurid light upon his position.

In Nána Farnavis he possessed an adviser who was to him all that Richelieu had been to Louis XIII of France, a custodian rather than a minister. The Nána was not unfriendly to Sindhia so long as their paths did not cross; but he was known as the 'Maráthá Machiavel'; and we can partly guess what that meant. For him, as for his august pupil, a tragic fall was waiting; but while the fall of the Prince was to be physical, that of the preceptor was to be moral and political—a fall from place and power and the esteem of his countrymen. But these things are beyond the present scope of our story. All that need here be noted is that the Nána and the Peshwá were so closely connected that one seemed necessary to the other; and that the ability and local influence of the Bráhman minister appeared to Sindhia to have assumed a character which menaced his position and called for personal efforts.

For it must always be remembered that Sindhia never meant to cut himself off from Poona. The roots of his power were in the Empire of which the Peshwá was the actual head; and it was only as a branch of that Empire that Sindhia ruled in Hindustán. Here the Nána was more than his equal in every respect, except, indeed, the important points of courage and character. Sindhia had a strong faith in the magnetism of his own genial nature in personal contact; and he recognised the importance of using that power on the young Peshwá before it was too late.

This explains the theatrical displays in the darbár-tent, as it accounts for the whole circumstances of the visit to Poona. There was to be one more battle before the final triumph; but it was intended to be a moral struggle between two men of almost equal power, one being braver, the other more unscrupulous.

What might have been the end if the struggle had been confined to the ordinary fields of political action, and fought out to the lawful conclusion, we have little or no material for deciding. Sindhia was nearly sixty; and, though his habits were simple and moderate, his life had been laborious; moreover, being unable, by reason of his lameness, to take much exercise, he had become somewhat unwholesomely corpulent. Against him he had not only the cool and crafty Bráhman minister, but Holkar smarting from late events, and perhaps as much inflamed by what he had done as by what he had suffered; for, after his defeat at Lakhairi, he had wasted Sindhia's estates in North Málwá and sacked his capital, Ujjain: Sindhia had exacted no penalty commensurate to these misdeeds; and Takúji had to pardon, if he could, both the injuries that he had inflicted and those that he had endured. Lastly, Sindhia was coldly regarded, if not positively disliked, by the knot of proud but needy warriors of the old school, who grieved at the abandonment of old Maráthá ways, and grudged the favour and employment bestowed upon so many foreigners. Men of that stamp were also particularly offended by the adoption of Muhammadan customs and the pretended humility by which Sindhia vainly sought to veil his pride.

That by such affectations as those displayed in the darbárs of June, 1792, Sindhia imposed upon his opponents is not to be readily supposed; but such a line of conduct was more likely to please—if not to blind—the youthful Peshwá, immature in experience of mankind and chafing under a somewhat austere control. Flattered by the attentions of his distinguished subordinate—Sindhia had insisted on accepting investiture from the Peshwá of the office of Deputy-Vicegerent—the young ruler was further won by Sindhia's frank, unreserved manners. He soon made the Patel his favourite and constant companion in those field-sports and open-air pursuits for which the grave and sedentary Nána was both unwilling and unfit. But that astute Bráhman watched these doings with unrelaxing vigilance; and it is related that happening to be alone on the water with the Peshwá one day he took occasion to remonstrate with his master in the most serious terms upon his favour to the intruder and his growing neglect of national manners and usages. When all his arguments seemed vain, he concluded by tendering his resignation of office with tears. It was on hearing of this interview that Sindhia ordered down the additional force which was sent to Poona under Perron.

But the contest was destined to a sudden end. On the 12th of February, 1794, it was announced that Sindhia had died of fever at a suburb of Poona called Wanaoli. The cause was said to be this; but there is no record of previous illness. The usually well-informed and contemporaneous author of the *Táríkh-i-Muzafari* gives a detailed account, according to which the Patel had been waylaid the evening before by an armed gang employed for the purpose by the Nána—who had certainly good reason to wish for his removal. It is stated, further, that Sindhia and his attendants made such a stout defence that the assailants were driven off; but the Chief sustained wounds of such severity as to cause his death next day. Such an incident was not unusual in Maráthá politics; many years after, the assassination of Gangadhar Shástri brought the Peshwáship to the ground.

Grant Duff, however, makes no direct reference to the rumour; only remarking that 'the death of Madhoji was an event of great political importance, as he was inimical to the overgrown ascendency of the Brahmins.'

The same judicious authority goes on to say of Mádhava that he was 'of a manly simplicity of character which led him to despise equally the trappings of state and the allurements of luxury.' It is evident that he was guided in his conduct by principles drawn from his own observation and judgment. Though by no means identified with the Conservative party, he really followed in the footsteps of his forefathers in being content with the substance of power without caring to drape himself in its robes. Instances of this Maráthá characteristic are given by Sir John Malcolm in describing the manner in which the early chiefs of the tribe obtained some of their territories. Thus, to cite but one example, we may take the province of Málwá—so often mentioned in this narrative. It was, as has been already stated, a region wrested from the Empire by the Peshwá Bálají Bájí Ráo after the first Nizám had left it when he set off to possess himself of the Haidarábád country. It was at first, indeed, held by a Hindu Viceroy under an appointment from Delhi. In 1732 the Peshwá effected an entrance by the connivance of some of the inhabitants. The Court of Delhi attempted negotiations, of which the ultimate result was that the Peshwá consented to administer the province as a feudatory of the Emperor. But the actual possession was by him apportioned between Malhárji Holkar and Ránojí Sindhia; while a formal deed was executed in which the Peshwá covenanted to hold the country for the Crown. And the actual possessors, the two Chiefs above-named, pledged themselves as security for his fealty; agreeing that, in case of his not conducting himself as a good and obedient Viceroy, they themselves would become the Peshwá's enemies. Yet all this did not prevent these two Chiefs from sharing the power and profit, as servants of the Peshwá, to whom they paid the surplus revenues.

Mádhava Sindhia, therefore, only acted on the example of his father, in purchasing the reality of power by a show of subordination, when he ruled Hindustán under the guise of a menial servant. So long as he grasped the substantial advantages, he was willing to be called the Peshwá's shoe-bearer and representative. But where he differed from his predecessors was in the intellectual vigour and unswerving constancy of purpose by which he clung to his advantages, when once obtained, and utilised them for further progress.

The point of this goes far below the surface, and enables us to perceive an essential peculiarity which Mádhava Sindhia shares with a very few great men. We are reminded of the occasional histrionisms of Oliver Cromwell and Lord Chatham, who were not above the production of stage effects and the use of theatrical properties. Yet neither of them was the dupe of his own performances, displayed for the behoof of a victorious army or a legislative chamber. We need not, then, think the less of Sindhia for his: he never forgot his real object, even in the very midst of his assumed humility. Nor was he of a hypocritical nature. If he offered to others the gauds that he himself despised, he did so quite openly; and never pretended to value those things that others were willing to accept as quit-rents of reality. The only mistake with which he can be fairly charged in this direction was that he seems to have somewhat underrated the intelligence of his public; and he sometimes overdid self-effacement until what was intended to disarm suspicion ended by increasing its force.

Another drawback in his character has been already noticed. If his natural good spirits made him active and buoyant in adverse fortune, they certainly led him to overstep the bounds of caution when all seemed to be going well.

Lastly, it must be admitted that his political conduct was not always very scrupulous. His tergiversations, when Raghuba, the Gloucester of Poona, was aiming at the Peshwáship, were not creditable. If the crimes of that unscrupulous Pretender were to be overlooked at all, a high-minded man would have at least been consistent in his support, and would not have withheld it when it was most required. Later on, Sindhia appears to have condoned the murder of Afrasyáb Khán, if he did not cause it; there is, at least, no record of the punishment of the murderer, who was well-known, and who took refuge in his camp. Twice he tried, in crooked ways, to see whether he could presume on the favour of the British authorities to wring from them the tribute of Bengal. In that demand he had a fair ground to go upon, and he need not have been in such a hurry with his absolute, and somewhat abject, disavowals.

To say that, in estimating a man placed as Sindhia was, we ought to avoid applying tests furnished by modern European manners is to lay down the tritest of platitudes. Nevertheless it is sometimes useful to recall the recollection of such truisms; and in this particular case to do so may act as a not superfluous caution. Indeed, even in more civilised times and more pretentious societies, the virtue of statesmen seems exposed to peculiar trials: 'Politics have a morality of their own,' said a German of distinction (Baron Beust) not many years ago; and Abraham Lincoln has been a rarer type in our own day than Napoleon III. Most certainly, in the India of Sindhia's time, men who came to the front in public affairs were usually either rogues or ruffians. Think of Ghází-ud-dín murdering his inoffensive Emperor and organising the plunder of his own subjects; of Ghulám Kádir's outrages in the Delhi palace, and Raghuba's murders in his own family at Poona: yet these men were countenanced as long as they were strong, and only failed when they attempted things beyond their powers.* Najíb-ud-daulá and Mírzá Najaf Khán, indeed, were at once respectable and successful men; but they were no more than the inevitable 'exceptions that prove the rule.' Amongst Asiatic public men, at least, there is no other name that can be fairly matched with that of Mádhava Sindhia: and even to these he was superior, alike in the scale of his success and in the qualities of his head and heart. Of this superiority, indeed, the above narrative, collected from many and varied sources, has afforded abundant proof[1].

Recollections gathered and recorded during the generation that succeeded throw a fuller light upon his personal character, and confirm the estimate derived from his actions. The general result is pleasing, if not wholly admirable. Clear in the conception of reasonable projects, he was bold and prudent in their realisation without yielding completely to the peculiar temptations of his place and time. In a scene of barbarous anarchy, when all the bonds of society seemed to be unloosed, he was amiable, courteous, and free from cruelty. Although his natural disposition was tenacious to the verge of vindictiveness, he kept it under and gradually cured its faults. We have seen how, in 1772, he pressed for vengeance against Najíb-ud-daulá and the Rohillás, preferring to withdraw for a time from the scene of his ambitious projects rather than be a party to their pardon or a willing waiver of revenge. If we contrast his almost

[1] See list of authorities. Mádhava was admired by men so diverse as Malcolm, Grant Duff, and de Boigne, by the depositaries of Maráthá tradition and the writers of Muhammadan history.

contemptuous condonation of Holkar's mischievous and malicious behaviour in 1792 we shall have some means of measuring the moral advance that he had made in less than a score of years. Thus we see that he not only overcame trials from without but trials from within also; and amongst the latter must be reckoned a natural infirmity of temper. For, if a certain endurance of resentment was a quality not without its uses in such a career as he had adopted, and almost essential to an amiable honest man surrounded by rascals, yet the unusual swiftness of anger by which, in this case, it was accompanied must have been a grievous stumbling-block. Of anger, as of money, it may be a general law that what is soon got is soon dissipated; but here the law would not apply: Sindhia was easily provoked, and not easily appeased.

But, if he seldom forgave an injury he never forgot a benefit: if he was severe in punishment, when punishment seemed requisite, he was not implacable or given to cause needless pain; while, in conferring rewards for service rendered, his gratitude admitted neither stint nor oblivion. Consequently, he was served with fidelity and affection: and his wishes were consulted even when he was dead and unable to enforce them. It is impossible to read the memoirs of de Boigne without seeing how great a part of Sindhia's success was due to the admiration inspired by his moral character, and the confidence with which his subordinates trusted to his consistency of conduct, good faith, and tenacity of purpose. He was good-humoured, if not exactly good-tempered; and his countenance, in spite of an unusually dark complexion, was full of amiability and intelligence; this expression was happily caught by a young Italian artist—name unrecorded—who painted Sindhia's portrait at Poona shortly before his death. This picture—now in the possession of the Right Honourable Sir M. Grant Duff—is an oil-painting, about 2 ft. by 1½, and is firmly drawn though somewhat cold in colour: it only shows the head and shoulders, and leaves the impression that the corpulence of the body could not have been excessive. Sindhia's manners were such as this portrait would suggest, frank and unaffected, in spite of the theatrical displays that he sometimes thought necessary for specific purposes.

His personal habits were simple and abstemious. Better educated than was usual among men of his class, he was not only able to read and write, but was a good accountant, and had a colloquial knowledge of Persian and Urdu. He was versed in business, and, without caring for the details either of war or civil administration, invariably chose good agents, whom he trusted thoroughly, and who repaid him for his confidence. As in Hindustán he was thoroughly well served by General de Boigne, so in Central India the officers whom he employed at Ujjain and Gwalior—where he was unable, for the most part, to inspect or control—were not less successful in fighting his battles and managing his affairs. The writer of these pages was informed by that eminent Maráthá statesman, the Hon. Sir Dinkar Ráo, that it was a tradition in high Poona society, handed down from aged men who had known Mádhava, that he was an excellent and indulgent master: unforgiving only towards officers who showed cowardice in battle. To all others his favour was equal, solely apportioned to merit without regard to creed, caste, or colour. By such a system men's hearts are won and great States founded; especially in the East, where despotic power usually leads to caprice, and caprice engenders distrust, discontent, bad service, and, ultimately, revolt and ruin.

The best proof that we are not over-estimating the merits of Mádhava Sindhia is to be found in the troubles which befel his successor. Dying without issue and without having performed any formal act of adoption, he left the power that he had founded to be exercised by the most capable of the family, designating as his heir a youth of fifteen. This was Daulat Ráo, a son of his youngest nephew, Anandi Ráo: and it is a remarkable sign of the respect and regard that had been inspired by the old man that this untried youth was instantly accepted in conformity with the great-uncle's orally-expressed wishes, and in despite of a strong opposition from the late Chief's widow. 'All the dependents of Sindhia's family,' we are told, 'and the other Maráthá authorities, sent their congratulations; so that this youth, who had hardly attained his fifteenth year, became undisputed heir to the extensive realms of Mahadajee' (Grant Duff, iii. 91).

That Mádhava died childless and without adopting a son to perform his obsequies will, to those who know the Hindu feeling on such subjects, appear a final proof of the originality of the man and of his superiority to the prejudices of his age and country. Even to this day the Hindus preserve that belief in the necessity of funeral rites for the repose of an ancestral soul which was becoming obsolete in Europe before the Christian era began. Hence a Hindu who sees himself approaching his end without heirs of his body, usually adopts a substitutive heir to do all that is considered needful for the preservation of the family and, still more, for the maintenance of his own personal welfare in the world of spirits. It is only by a somewhat earnest consideration of this principle that we come to realise the independent nature of a man who was indifferent to his own spiritual welfare, and was content to leave the succession to his power by word of mouth, and as a trust reposed in his officers. Mádhava, evidently enough, cared as little for the terrors of the next world as for the pomps of the world that he knew. But he instructed his people as to the choice of a successor; and, when he was dead, the son of Anandi Ráo was grafted on the main stem, in conformity with the indications of the deceased ruler, and as effectually, for all practical purposes, as if all the Shástris in Poona had borne part in a formal adoption. That the choice was not more fortunate must be ascribed to the nature of the field.

It is no part of our task to trace in detail the

results of this: but a few of them may be profitably noted in illustration of the peculiar difficulties of the position that we have been considering, and of the peculiar qualities implied in the fact that Mádhava had overcome them. The difference which separated the prudent soldier, who knew his own mind and made his own fortune, from the vacillating youth bred in indulgence and attentive to obsequious followers, soon became apparent. Mádhava, as we have partly seen, had always proposed to himself the difficult but singularly original scheme of creating a position, in which he should combine the delights of independent power with the advantages to be derived from continuing a member of the confederacy of which the Peshwá was President. To do this he found it necessary to rule and fight with unremitting vigour in Hindustán while he trimmed the diplomatic balance at Poona: further, contriving to stand well with the Nána, be respected by Holkar, and preserve the friendly neutrality of the British. But he abstained from doing violence to Maráthá loyalty or drawing his sword in quarrels about the succession; he did not resist the British when he found them to be in earnest; and he never drove Holkar to despair.

But when he was dead the inheritor of his power proved quite unable so to manage the mighty engine. First, the unfortunate young Peshwá committed suicide, dashing himself to death as a way of escape from the Nána's tutelage. Then Daulat Ráo took up the question of the succession, now on one side, now on the other. At last he was induced to declare for Bájí Ráo, the son of Raghuba the old Pretender; and then, when Bájí became Peshwá, Daulat Ráo aided and abetted in the forcible seizure of the Nána, who ended his days in disgrace, if not in actual captivity. Then Daulat Ráo proceeded to alienate public opinion by the ill-treatment of his predecessor's widows. Then he proceeded to appropriate the Nána's landed estate, and so provoked a quarrel with the Peshwá, three of whose ministers he seized and put to death. In regard to Holkar a like policy of implacable hostility was adopted by Daulat Ráo, leading to much bloodshed and general havoc. But his most conspicuous folly was shown in his dealings with the British.

Of that power Mádhava had always entertained a discreet awe. Even in their lowest depression—before Goddard had come into the West and retrieved the national reputation—Mádhava had appreciated the 'majesty with which the British soldier fights.' After the disaster of Egerton and Carnac, Mádhava said, in a low voice, to one of the envoys suing for salvation at Wadgáon: 'What soldiers yours are! Their line is like a red brick wall; and when one falls another steps into the gap. I hope some day to fight on the same side' (Grant Duff). Sir J. Malcolm, who relates the anecdote with some variation, says that he added, 'And such are the troops that I should like to have.' So Pyrrhus praised the valour of the Roman soldiers after he had beaten them at Heraclea;

and, like the Epirote leader, Sindhia never afterwards willingly quarrelled with the State which owned such material of war. He did his best, indeed, to imitate them; yet neither he nor his able General ever exaggerated the merits of the imitation. Never to quarrel with the British, and rather disband all his new-model men than engage them in a conflict with that power, such was the advice handed down to Daulat Ráo through General de Boigne. But the General left India in 1797, and was succeeded in the command of the army by Perron, a Frenchman of low birth, narrow training, and a full share of vulgar prejudice against perfidious Albion. The end was swift disaster.

Daulat Ráo was, perhaps, the best successor that Mádhava could select; but he was soon to prove himself unequal, intellectually as well as morally, to the due maintenance and employment of his uncle's complicated system. He posed as the swordsman of the Peshwá rather than as the Deputy-Vicegerent of the Emperor; filling his armies with foreign mercenaries and choosing incapable advisers often of the worst character and antecedents; shocking public opinion by outrageous conduct, and alienating his best Maráthá lieutenants. Towards the Court and Cabinet of Poona he was habitually insolent and sometimes violent; he plundered the city, confined or slew eminent public men, propagated feud and assassination in the House of Holkar, and fatally weakened the coherence of the whole Maráthá confederation. Lastly, he proceeded to extremities with the long-suffering East India Company, and hastened to wreck and ruin like an ill-steered vessel on a lee shore. The inferiority of his trained troops to those on whose pattern they were formed justified the forebodings of Maráthá Conservatives, confirmed by the opinion of that wise and warlike Englishman, who 'clashed with his fiery few, and won' at Asai. Yet, injudicious as was the provoking of that conflict, the illustrious critic could not have meant that Mádhava's original introduction of discipline was of itself an evil; but only that it was so if it caused presumption and led to an unequal collision. Had the Maráthá armies continued the guerrilla warfare of their ancestors they might have given more trouble to the Wellesleys and to Lake, who, it must be admitted, were able to make short work of their battalions and their batteries when it came to a serious conflict. Nevertheless, the subsequent fate of the Pindárís—who adopted the old Maráthá strategy—serves to show that in any case the British must have ultimately prevailed. Nothing could well have seemed more formidable, in its way, than the combination that awaited Lord Moira in 1815. He had sent four columns to the northward to attack Nepál, and three of them had ignominiously failed. The Court of Directors had sent out stringent orders forbidding him 'to engage in plans of offensive operations against the Pindarees, either with a view to their extirpation or in anticipation of expected danger.' His designs were opposed by the most experienced members of his Council. Daulat Ráo Sindhia was hostile, and occupying Central India, in alliance with the Rájá of Nágpur, and at the head of 60,000 men. Bájí Ráo adopted a threatening attitude, and was known to be encouraging the enemy. At the *dasahra* of 1815 the largest body of Pindárís took the field that had ever been assembled. A body of 8000 of them crossed the Narbadá and devastated the Nizám's territories as far south as the Krishna river. A large division poured down on the British districts of the Northern Sirkárs, and sacked the civil station of Gantur, laying waste the surrounding country: the loss of life was considerable, the loss of property was reckoned at twenty-five *lákhs* of rupees. The agents of the Pindárí Chiefs openly boasted, in Sindhia's darbár, that they would send 50,000 men to carry fire and sword to Calcutta. Their total number was estimated at nearly 100,000: the scene of action extended from the Ganges to the Krishna, and from Cawnpur to Gujarát. To add to the anxieties of the time cholera broke out in the camps of the British and caused a loss—including camp-followers—of 20,000 men. Bájí Ráo took the field with 18,000 soldiers and attacked the British Resident at Poona; the Rájá of Nágpur followed his example: in the middle of October, 1817, the joint forces of the enemy amounted to more than 150,000 horse and foot, with 500 pieces of artillery.

All these perils were dispersed in four months: the power of Daulat Ráo was isolated by able manœuvres;

the army of Holkar had ceased to exist; the Peshwá, Báji Ráo, was a fugitive; the Pindárí leaders had been abandoned by their followers and had been forced to surrender, or had perished in their own jungles.

It is therefore evident that no species of native warfare was proof against European resources, and that Mádhava Sindhia had made no mistake in founding his ambitious schemes on a force of regular troops, disciplined and commanded by European officers: matched against the old Asiatic systems of warfare he had completely succeeded. The mistake was that of his heir in thinking that this necessarily second-class army could prevail over the first-class army on which it was modelled. The same mistake was afterwards made by the Sikhs; and, though made with every advantage of material and men, ended, after a hard-fought struggle, in the like result.

After all, the great question for modern readers is, What, intentionally and unintentionally, did Mádhava Sindhia do; and what was the ultimate bearing of the events that we have been tracing on the progress of the British Empire in India? We have seen that the circumstances which led to the Treaty of Salbái established in Mádhava's mind a permanent respect for the military qualities of the British. Of their diplomatic abilities he entertained a lower opinion, even when represented by Warren Hastings. A singular instance of this is related by Grant Duff. Hastings was known, about that time, to be contemplating the despatch of a Mr. Malet, as an envoy to the Court of the Peshwá at Poona; and Mádhava's objection is worthy of attention. He used no threats, nor did he treat the proposal to treat direct with his suzerain as a menace on the part of the British Government. Yet he was strongly opposed to what he considered as a dangerous interference. He therefore represented that the mission was unnecessary, for the curious reason that he, Sindhia, was the true representative of British interests with the Maráthá confederacy. The plea was rejected; but it is sufficiently remarkable that it should have been seriously urged. He was, in fact, much employed and trusted in the negotiations; and the profit that he was enabled to derive from them made of the resulting treaty the opportunity which led to the assurance of his power in Hindustán.

After he had surmounted all his difficulties, and when, in 1789, he finally became at once the master of the Empire and the umpire in Maráthá politics, he had a real influence on British progress. If it cannot be positively said that he restrained the Nána and Holkar from attacking the British and their allies, he at least found them occupation. When Lord Cornwallis was being drawn into war with Tipú, in 1790, Sindhia abstained from forming any combination against him, and proffered assistance which was, somewhat ungraciously, declined. Indeed, it is plain that his power and influence were always regarded with anxiety. The records of the Supreme

Government of those days abound in signs of watchful suspicion. In the opinion of Grant Duff—and there is no better authority—that attitude was without just cause.

We must therefore conclude our study by a word of just acknowledgment. Alike by what he did and by what he refrained from doing, by his conquests in war and by his administration in peace, Mádhava Sindhia approved himself a wise and useful ruler: and he was both a precursor and a factor in the establishment of a rule stronger and more beneficent than his own.

INDEX

THE END.